Change It!

If you want to change your life, you have to *change your life!*

Bill Quain, Ph.D.
Doug Price

⊔ **Wales Publishing**

DEDICATION

We dedicate this book to our mutual friend, the late Phil Mogle who understood the power of change better than most people. Phil's legacy lives on today through the lives of his widow Sandee and sons Matthew and Mark.

ACKNOWLEDGEMENTS

This book is a product of true collaboration by many people. We would like to acknowledge Jack and Elizabeth Parry, from Parry Design, for the book layout, graphics, and cover design. We also acknowledge Mark Hayes for editing the manuscript. We thank our wives Jeanne Quain and Kathy Price for proofreading and editing, ideas, and inspiration. Most importantly we acknowledge our children who teach us daily that the world is changing fast and we better get on board!

Change It!
Bill Quain, Ph.D. & Doug Price

Published by Wales Publishing Company
Ocean City, New Jersey

Wales Publishing Company is exclusively owned and operated by Bill Quain

www.quain.com

Cover design by Parry Design Studio, Inc. - www.parrydesign.com

Printed in the United States of America

First printing - January 2009

ISBN: 978-0-9785295-5-0

TABLE OF CONTENTS

IMPORTANT—Read This First

∾

WE WANT YOU TO UNDERSTAND three things about change, even before you read this book. These three tenets are so important, so fundamental, that we need to cover them in a special section of the book.

Look at this:

1. Change is Choice.

2. Change is *your* Choice.

3. If you work with other people, you need to make Change *their* Choice.

Pastor Rick Warren, author of *The Purpose Driven Life,* cleverly describes the problems that most people have with change by using the example of a boat on auto-pilot. According to Warren, many people try to make changes without adjusting the auto-pilot. They struggle to turn the wheel of the ship and put it on a new course. This causes a lot of tension. They are always fighting the wheel and trying to stay on the new course. Eventually the work, the tension, is just too much, they let go of the wheel, and the ship returns to its original course.

When we say that "Change is Choice" we aren't talking about choosing to turn the wheel; we want you to choose to change the autopilot. We are talking about a fundamental choice. You need to change your whole way of thinking. And if you work with others, you must help them change their way of thinking.

"But, I didn't choose this change, it was forced on me"

We hear this from people all the time, and this is the perfect place to overcome that excuse—right at the beginning of our book! Yes, you might be in the midst of a change you didn't create. However, everything you do after that change is your choice.

The way you react to change, the things you choose to do to manage it and grow with it are entirely up to you. "My boss is a jerk!" Okay, what are you going to do about it? "I am broke, and running out of money because I was laid off!" Okay, what are you going to do about it? What are you going to do so it doesn't happen again?

The choice is yours. Will you simply turn the wheel, and try to fight a losing battle, or will you learn to make fundamental changes that can make a real difference?

THE BOOK—THREE PARTS, THREE CHANGES

We divided this book into three parts: *Change Yourself, Change Others*, and *Change Everything*. There is a good reason why the parts are in this sequence. In order to get anything done, you must first make the fundamental choice to change. Just as importantly, you must help other people make the fundamental choice to change.

So, start with the last chapter first.

"What, is this a mistake? You just told me that the book has three parts! Shouldn't I start at the beginning?"

No, start at the end. Read Chapter 12 first, then the Introduction.

BACKWARDS DESIGN

In Part II, Change People, we introduce a concept called "Backwards Design." Basically, this concept shows you how to visualize the end result of your plans and strategies first, then work backwards from there so that everything you do leads to the desired outcomes. In this book, Chapter 12 is a summary, a recap of the major points of this book. In fact, we give you a list of the core principles and the major points at the beginning of Chapter 12. Next to each of those major points is a blank space.

We suggest the following:

Read the last chapter first. Then, as you are reading the book, look for the major points that are outlined in Chapter 12. In the blank space next to each major point, write the *page number* where the point is introduced in the book and any other page numbers that are important to the point.

WHY? Because we want you to make some fundamental changes. If you just read the book from the beginning to the end, you might be "fighting the wheel." We want you to visualize the entire process first, then start learning the principles one by one.

Folks, in the end, you will write to thank us! We aren't going to give you just some new ideas. We show you how to change the autopilot and make a permanent, meaningful difference in your life and the lives of others.

What is Change?

C‿◡

CONGRATULATIONS FOR PICKING UP THIS BOOK on change. You have made a decision to change your life, the lives of other people and the circumstances that surround you. Most people will tell you that the need for change in their life is obvious. They just don't know how to do it. This book will help answer your questions and give you a step-by-step process for changing yourself. You will also learn how to help other people change.

Let's begin with a definition of change.

Change is a relatively permanent shift or alteration of *beliefs, attitudes, habits, behaviors or processes* in response to anticipated risks and opportunities.

Sounds pretty involved doesn't it? Let's break it down because understanding change is so important.

Change is—

- **A relatively *permanent shift or alteration*** – Temporary changes don't concern us here! Don't worry about them. You don't need this book if you are thinking about making a short-term change, then returning to the old ways. In this book, we are talking about permanent changes that you will make or help others to make.

- **Of *beliefs, attitudes, habits, behaviors or processes*** – exactly what are you going to change? The most important thing you can change is your *belief* system. This is not easy. However, it is almost impossible to create sustained, effective change without altering your beliefs.

- In *response to anticipated risks and opportunities* – Change is a *response* mechanism. We make changes because of something that is happening around us. However, you don't need to actually wait for something to happen. The most successful people *anticipate* events that will occur and make changes in advance of the event. Hockey great Wayne Gretzky once said, "I skate to where the puck is going to be—not where it has been."

Keep in mind this book is about personal change—yours and others. It is not necessarily a management book for managing change in an organization. There are a ton of books on that subject already. We are going to show you how to make effective changes in your life. You will learn how to become more successful in three specific areas: money, health, and relationships. In the book we will refer to them as Money, Sunny, and Honey. Once you have learned to change yourself, we will show you how to help other people change.

Change is Continuous

We have some good news and some bad news about change. Actually, the good news and bad news are the same thing: change is continuous. It is always happening. External forces are always changing, so you must always be changing.

Much has been written about the continuous nature of change. We won't spend too much time on it here, because it really is pretty obvious. But we do want to share a fabulous insight attributed to the former CEO of Coca-Cola. It is found on a website called themanager. org. In a speech, the CEO of Coke said:

"Our research indicates the following:

A billion hours ago, man first appeared on the earth.

A billion minutes ago, Christianity first appeared.

A billion seconds ago, the Beatles performed on the Ed Sullivan Show.

A billion Cokes ago was yesterday morning!"

The CEO went on to say that Coca Cola wanted to make a change in this analogy. They wanted it to accurately read "A billion Cokes ago was *this* morning."

This anecdote illustrates two points. First, change is continuous. Second, successful companies (and the people in them) are continually changing. Coke could sit back and profit from the sale of a billion cokes per day. But instead, they chose to increase that number even more by making the necessary changes in their company.

Change is continuous, and if you do not continually change, you run the risk of falling behind. Too many people make one change in their life and then stop. This is dangerous! It is a great way to lose out on opportunities or to succumb to risks and threats.

THE PACE OF CHANGE IS ACCELERATING

Do we really need to spend time in this book convincing you that the pace of change is accelerating? Let's hope not! The speed of change should be perfectly obvious.

A few years ago, putting together a spreadsheet would have taken all day. Now, we expect everything instantly—or sooner. Why? *Because everything has changed.* Computers, the internet, and satellites make our lives so much easier—and they force change on us so much quicker.

It wasn't long ago that it was excusable to be late for a business appointment. People could say "I had trouble finding the address" or "I got stuck in traffic." These excuses don't even exist anymore. Your car's GPS system gives exact directions to any location. And that same GPS system should have automatic traffic updates with recommended alternate routes. Life comes at you quickly. Be ready.

CHANGE AND YOU

Okay, now you have the definition of change. And you know that it is continuous and accelerating. What does that mean for you?

It means that you need to establish some sort of change system to monitor opportunities and threats, and to either take advantage of them (opportunities) or avoid them (threats). It is simple. *Change It!* to stay out of trouble and to improve your life.

We will stress one thing again and again throughout this book. We are not interested in teaching *about* change. We want to show you how to take *advantage* of change to improve your life. And, we are going to show you how to use it in three specific areas. If you realize this, and that change is continuous and accelerating, you can continually improve your life—and get faster and faster results!

That is the power of this book. It is the power of understanding change. *Change It!* is the power we want to give you and have you give to others.

WRITER'S TIP ON HOW TO GET THE MOST OUT OF THE BOOK

This book is organized into three sections. Part One is how to change yourself. You are going to get a thorough understanding of how to recognize problems in your life. This is important because when you see the *Change It!* Program explained in Chapter Two, it will become clear what the consequences are for not recognizing problems that need to be acted upon.

Part Two is about how to change people. This is very important because you want to know how to help other people change by first becoming a change agent and then changing others' circumstances.

Part Three is how to change everything! We will take you through the key steps of innovation, creativity, and brainstorming. Why is this important? Because in order to effectively implement change, you need to do more than think outside the box—we suggest you *demolish* the box and always think "outside."

One of the important principles of this book is called "Backwards Design." You will read more about it in Chapter 7. In essence, it means to start at the end, not at the beginning. Our tip to you is this—in the spirit of "Backwards Design," go read Chapter 12 first. It provides you perspective on all the important principles of this book. We put a blank line next to each principle. To get the most out of the book, we suggest that as your read the book, use Chapter 12 to record the page numbers for each important principle. This way the book becomes a useful resource for you both now and in the future.

∾ Part I – Change Yourself

Remember, Change is Choice, and Change is *your* Choice. Everything starts with you. You need to learn how change works and how to initiate change strategies.

More importantly, you need to learn WHY you need to change.

In Part I, you get an introduction to the *Change It!* Program, and the three-part definition of a successful person. Use the program as a guide for change, and use the three-part definition of success as the reason to change.

If You Want to Change Your Life, You Have to Change Your Life

∾

HOW MANY LOTTERY WINNERS LOSE all their money and end up poor? More than you'd expect. What is truly amazing is how quickly these lucky winners go from being millionaires to being bankrupt. Some lottery winners actually lose it all within the first year. And it isn't just the money—that would be bad enough. The stories are terrible: bad financial decisions, broken families, lost relationships. Good friends and close family members can go crazy when they have even the possibility of getting their hands on free money. As one lottery winner put it, "The money changed everything."

Or did it?

In all the cases we have seen, where lottery winners go broke, there is one common theme. They were all poor *before* winning the money! When wealthy people win lotteries, they stay wealthy. When poor people win lotteries, many of them become poor again despite the enormous wealth that drops into their laps.

The lesson here isn't a money management lesson. It is a life lesson.

It isn't the circumstances around you that determine how successful you will be. It is what is *inside* you that makes the difference.

You are reading this book because you want something to be different. You want to make changes. But if you want to change your life, you have to change your life. That is the title of this chapter, and the theme of this book.

There are people who think that some *external* change would make their lives better. Many lottery players reason that way. They buy their tickets each week, thinking "If I could just win some money, I could live easier. I would get out of debt, drive a nice car, go on lots of vacations, and live the sweet life." They buy their tickets and hope. They go on about their lives, week after week, waiting for someone to pick a certain sequence of numbers out of a cage.

In the meantime, they keep on doing the same old things that made their life unsuccessful in the first place. They make bad decisions—or no decisions at all. They *hope* for things, but they don't *do* the things necessary to create success. Casinos and race tracks are full of people hoping things will change.

But waiting for things to change is not the same as actually changing. If you wait for some external force or set of circumstances to change your life, you will never truly change your life.

Become a Winner at the Start

Two men were watching the Tour de France on television. It was a brutally hot day in France, and the riders were sweating and tired.

"I don't understand why those riders would put themselves through all that trouble," said the first man. "They get on those bikes early in the morning and ride up and down mountains all day long. Then, they do it a second day, and a third. That race covers over 2,000 miles and lasts for three weeks."

"Well," said the second man. "The winner gets a lot of money, fantastic endorsements, and the admiration of millions of adoring fans."

"Oh" said the first man. "I understand why the *winner* does it. But why would all those other guys do it?"

And there is the lesson about winners. For them, life is worth the effort. For them, learning, making changes, working hard and staying in focus are worth it. But for everyone else, why bother?

In the Tour de France, there is only one winner. Only one person stands on that platform at the end of the day with his hands raised in triumph.

In life, anyone can be a winner. Anyone can triumph. There is no limit, no quota.

But if you don't intend to be a winner, then changing your life is not going to be worth it. You won't go through all the effort necessary, because the effort won't pay off.

Most people think the winners are declared at the conclusion of the race, so they spend their whole lives waiting for the end. They think "I will make a fast sprint at the end and finish strong. I will save my effort for when it really counts—at the end."

This is exactly the wrong idea. The time to put effort into the race, or the game, or into life, is at the beginning. You need to make changes now so you will have the things you want later. You can't win at the end if you haven't been a winner all along.

This is one of the major points of our book. We are going to teach you how to make changes in your life now—not at the end. You won't make the changes after everything has played out. You won't be encouraged to "wait and see." Instead, we are going to show you how to take charge of your life and make things happen today.

EXTERNAL FORCES MAGNIFY YOUR LIFE

Your life is your life and you made it that way. If it is good, it is because you did the things necessary to make it good. If it is bad, it is not because someone else did something. It is because *you* made it bad. External forces only magnify your positive or negative attitudes, your beliefs and actions.

For example, when those lottery winners went broke after receiving millions of dollars, it was because they did not know how to create wealth or even how to handle it. Their problem wasn't a lack of money. No, they had a lack of money because they had problems!

Their problems were pretty basic: They had never learned to make money. They had never learned to set goals and stick to a plan. Also, none of their friends, family or acquaintances was wealthy. So when the lottery money dropped into their lives, they had no clue how to handle it.

Now, they could have said, "I have no point of reference for this wealth. I need to get some good advice from people who know money. I need to look around and figure out how to make changes so the rest of my life will be better."

Of course, not everyone who wins the lottery ends up losing all their money. In fact, some people go from poverty to wealth and stay there! But these long term winners come from one of two groups. First, they were either wealthy (or at least money-savvy) to begin with. Or second, they *changed* quickly and learned how to handle their money.

INTERNAL CHANGE VERSUS EXTERNAL CHANGE

During the course of your life—both personal and professional— things are going to happen. You will lose a job, get sick, have a boss that hates you, meet people who will try to cheat you, and so forth. You will also have great things happen, such as meeting a wonderful person, making great friends, enjoying good health, and maybe even winning the lottery. You will be faced with many external changes during the course of your life. No problem. These are just technicalities. They aren't YOU. They are the *outside* world.

But your success should always be based solely on your internal preparation and the desire *inside* you to win. If you prepare yourself, you can conquer many adversities. You will be in a position to take advantage of opportunities. If your core values and practices are sound, you will be able to achieve your dreams despite almost any outside force.

This is the difference between internal and external change. The world around you is going to deliver positive and negative. If you read this book, you can minimize negative effects and magnify positive effects. Internal change is a series of steps to prepare you to win. It begins with dream building and goal setting. And it never ends.

THE ONE-AND-DONE MISTAKE

We see it all the time. Someone makes a change, and then stops! People erroneously see change as a One-and-Done process. The fact is that true change is an ongoing, dynamic and *growing* process.

In the United States, the majority of young adults go to college. After 12 years of general education, they enter a university and choose a major. In that major—whether it is business, music, nursing, and so forth—they learn all the things necessary to get a job. Then, when they get out of college, they stop their formal learning! They spend the rest of their lives working. This is a One-and-Done change

However, the fact that they learned a *subject* rather than a process is a dangerous plan of action. There is no problem with learning a subject. As long as the students understand that what they know about a subject is only what is known today. It may not be what is known tomorrow. In fact, it is *probably* not what will be known tomorrow.

The world is full of examples of people who only know one way of doing things. Have you ever heard people say, "Well, I'll try it once, but we have always done it this way"? In other words, they make a one time change, but chances are they are unwilling to sustain the new change or unable to make an additional change.

A classic example takes place with New Year's resolutions. Health club memberships soar in January when people make a resolution to get fit and start a new exercise program. After a while they become bored with the new program. They need to make another change and hire a personal trainer or sign up for a regular class, so the resolutions never really end.

GROWTH VERSUS PERFECTION

Many people see change as a task rather than a process. They want to get it right, and then gain closure. All done! They are looking for perfection rather than growth.

In this book, we are going to help you start the growth process. You will most likely never be finished. Remember: If you want to change your life, you have to change your life.

The One-and-Done crowd wants to set a task, complete it, and then just do the same thing over and over again. While that might be nice, and convenient, it doesn't work in reality. In fact, we can't think of a single instance where the One-and-Done theory applies.

FROM ONE-AND-DONE TO START-AND-GROW

It is more important to establish *a system for change* than to make a change. Most anyone can make a change. Sometimes, the pressure is so great that you absolutely must change. This doesn't take much talent.

Think about a marital relationship that is on the brink of dissolving because one spouse is always working. Finally, in desperation, the other spouse lays down an ultimatum: "Either you spend more time at home or I am leaving you." The spouse makes some changes and the marriage is saved. Or is it?

Of course, we applaud the person for making a change. However, be assured that they will have to make many more changes in order to keep their marriage together. And, don't wait until the pressure is so strong that it reaches a breaking point before making change. Again, this does not take talent. It takes problem recognition and ongoing growth—Start-and-Grow.

ENJOY THE JOURNEY

Personal growth is a wonderful thing. It is a great way to change. It is a never ending journey, not a destination in and of itself.

"A journey that never ends?" you are saying. "Who wants that? It sounds like too much trouble."

It certainly can be at times. It requires you to think, learn, and grow. Most people never even do the first thing—think—let alone the other two! But we have some great news for you. Learning to start and grow—rather than change and stop—will bring you terrific rewards in life. And the more you change and grow, the richer the rewards become. Ultimately, you will help change others.

Whether you are growing in wealth, health or relationships, your rewards get bigger and richer. We can make you a promise: look at change as a journey and you will live a richer life than you can imagine.

So, get over the One-and-Done mindset. Again: If you want to change your life, you have got to change your life. Get on the Start-and-Grow track. The journey is worth it. We promise!

Note from Bill and Doug

The big idea from this chapter is to *start* each endeavor as a winner. Don't wait until the end and start a big push. This is a clear difference between a winner and a person who is just plain annoying! Change starts when change starts - not when you want to finish. Change is a "start it!" tool, not a "finish it!" tool.

CHAPTER 2

Creating an Environment of Change

∽

There Is No "I" In C-H-A-N-G-E

HAVE YOU EVER HEARD THE EXPRESSION "There is no 'I' in T-E-A-M"? Sure you have. It is one of those things people say all the time. It means that in a team, no one is supposed to shine. Everyone is equal. Everyone puts in an equal amount of effort, according to their abilities.

What a stupid expression! We hate it! Does that surprise you? You are probably thinking "Wait a minute. You guys are authors. You are supposed to love those kinds of expressions." We do love catchy phrases and sayings—"If you want to change your life you have to change your life" is a favorite.

But "There is no 'I' in T-E-A-M" just drives us crazy.

Why? Because people use it too often as an excuse. Bosses use it whenever they don't want to recognize the outstanding effort of a team member. Average or slightly below average team members use it to excuse their performance, as in "I don't try to outperform anyone. I am a member of a team."

You will see when reading this book that we believe there is an "I" in everything! Every change starts with an "I." Without the "I" nothing would happen. If you don't take personal responsibility for your life, nothing good will come to pass. Results come from "I." "Achieve" and "Win" certainly have an "I" in them!

Now, if you are one of those people who say "There is no 'I' in TEAM," you might also be tempted to say "There is no 'I' in CHANGE."

And while, grammatically, you are right, you are wrong to think that saying makes sense.

To make it easier for you, we named this book *"Change It!"*. *Change It!* does have an "I." In fact, it has both an "I" and an exclamation point!

INTRODUCING THE *CHANGE IT!* PROGRAM

We are going to show you a fantastic model that serves as the foundation of our program for this book. By definition, a model is a system that serves as a plan for something not yet produced. We want you to see how this model or program can produce sustained change in your life.

So, how do you go about instituting some sort of sustained change in your life? In order for change to effectively take hold, all six of these components need to be in place:

PROBLEM RECOGNITION

+

SHARED DREAM

+

INCENTIVE TO CHANGE

+

CAPACITY TO CHANGE

+

PRESSURE TO CHANGE

+

ACTIONABLE FIRST STEPS

=

CHANGE

The *Change It!* Program is simple, but not easy. It is simple to understand, but not so easy to implement. On pages 30 and 31, you will see a graphic showing how our *Change It!* Program works. Each component of the program is defined to show the cause and effect of each condition in the personal implementation stage. To give you a really good understanding, let's take a step-by-step look at the program.

Step One: Problem Recognition

∿ If you do not identify the problem, a change dies right away. There is no chance for change to take place if you don't recognize some sort of problem from the very start.

There must be a realization that the current condition is different than the desired condition, and tacit approval is unacceptable. The word "tacit" implies *something not spoken but approved by actions.* Tacit approval is the realization you know something isn't right but you accept it as is. The opposite of tacit is "explicit" which is the realization *you must act to achieve a new desired condition and you do so.*

Step Two: Shared Dream

It is said that whatever your mind can conceive and believe, the body can achieve. Just ask any world-class entertainer or athlete how important is to have a belief in himself or herself. With that said,

∿ If everything is in place except a shared dream, the outcome is a fast start that fizzles out because no one understands what success will ultimately look like.

change can be hard and uncomfortable. For sustained change to take hold in your life, you need to have big dreams and then be willing to share those dreams with others you trust. It is a smart to align yourself with others who are changing or have experienced personal change themselves. The reason sharing is so very important is the power that comes in telling others why your dreams are beneficial to you and ultimately to them.

Step Three: Incentive to Change

Incentives to change flow out of the shared dream. The incentive gets to the heart of all the potential rewards for you—so write them all down. It is truly worth documenting this list of rewards. And while you are at it, include all the incentives for other people as your dreams come

> ∽ If everything is in place except the incentive to change, the outcome will be slowed down. Without shared incentives people do not grasp what is in it for them.

true. Our human nature dictates that people need to know what's in it for them.

Step Four: Capacity to Change

> ∽ If everything is in place except capacity to change, the result is anxiety and frustration. It is frustrating when you don't have the resources necessary for change.

Capacity to change flows out of the shared dream and incentive to change. Capacity is the collective knowledge and resources needed to achieve sustainable change. Ask some tough questions, because you'll be facing both internal and external capacity issues. Is your heart ready to change, or is this simply a mental exercise? The gap between your head and heart makes all the difference in the world. If your heart is not ready for change, the chances are that any change you make will be temporal. If you are in need of external knowledge or resources, think about where to turn to seek out potential role models for assistance. And always remember to share your dreams and incentives with those you trust.

Step Five: Pressure to Change

Pressure to change reveals how to create change through sustained action. Do not avoid pressure—embrace it! Only the brave and bold will inflict pressure on themselves. They are the same ones that will actually accomplish change. For example, there is a popular television show in the United States called *The Biggest Loser*. The show features people committed to losing an enormous amount of weight—on national television. Imagine the pressure of standing on the scale every week for millions of people to judge your progress!

> ∽ If everything is in place except pressure to change, your dream just rests on your mental or physical "in-basket" and gets buried by the next task that takes precedence.

Applying pressure on yourself is a sign of maturity. Picture digging a well before you need the water. Or picture taking your dream out of the computer recycle bin and going public with it. Pressure can be as simple as making a declaration of your intent to change. You can also develop pressure by choosing whom you associate with. To increase your wealth, hang out with wealthy people. Going public and sharing dreams and incentives creates a natural pressure.

Step Six: Actionable First Steps

> ∽ If everything is in place except actionable first steps, you make a false or even haphazard start because you don't know where to begin.

This places the *Change It!* Program into motion. Actionable first steps are a result of combining the problem recognition, dreams, incentives, capacity and pressure. The first steps should be so easy to do that it is almost impossible to not act. Picture a nation's military amassed on an enemy's border ready for action. After all the preparation and planning, it is very hard for the military to "stand down" and not take action.

If this *Change It!* Program makes sense to you, we encourage you to personally adapt it. Perhaps it might explain why you are "stuck in the mud" in an attempt to change.

Truly, all six components of the *Change It!* Program must be in place for sustainable change to occur in a timely and effective manner.

Change It! Program

Problem Recognition **+** Shared Dream **+** Incentive To Change **+** Capacity To Change

~~Problem Recognition~~ **+** Shared Dream **+** Incentive To Change **+** Capacity To Change

Problem Recognition **+** ~~Shared Dream~~ **+** Incentive To Change **+** Capacity To Change

Problem Recognition **+** Shared Dream **+** ~~Incentive To Change~~ **+** Capacity To Change

Problem Recognition **+** Shared Dream **+** Incentive To Change **+** ~~Capacity To Change~~

Problem Recognition **+** Shared Dream **+** Incentive To Change **+** Capacity To Change

Problem Recognition **+** Shared Dream **+** Incentive To Change **+** Capacity To Change

$+$ **Pressure To Change** $+$ **Actionable First Steps** $=$ **Change**

$+$ **Pressure To Change** $+$ **Actionable First Steps** $=$ **Do What You Have Always Done**

$+$ **Pressure To Change** $+$ **Actionable First Steps** $=$ **Fast Start That Fizzles**

$+$ **Pressure To Change** $+$ **Actionable First Steps** $=$ **Slow, Gradual Change**

$+$ **Pressure To Change** $+$ **Actionable First Steps** $=$ **Anxiety and Frustration**

$+$ ~~**Pressure To Change**~~ $+$ **Actionable First Steps** $=$ **Buried by the next Fire**

$+$ **Pressure To Change** $+$ ~~**Actionable First Steps**~~ $=$ **False, Haphazard Start**

BILL QUAIN AND THE *CHANGE IT!* MODEL

Problem Recognition & Shared Dream

"One day as I watched a yacht sail by, my dream became 'to live on the water and be financially independent.' Being handicapped with deteriorating eyesight, my choices were becoming more limited. My dream was to actually have more choices in life—not less. I shared this dream with my wife Jeanne and two business partners, Ron and Sharon Browning."

Incentive to Change

"My incentive to change was to actually rid myself of the disincentives in my life. I wanted to become independent and take control of my life. As a college professor, I grew tired of being the best at my profession but being treated just like every other faculty member. I also wanted to take control of transportation for myself in light of my deteriorating eyesight."

Capacity to Change

"I had already written a few books and was doing a fair amount of outside speaking as a faculty member. There were friends of mine who were already successful writers that would share their knowledge with me on how to write and market books. Also, my parents owned a small publishing company so they were a great resource. I had a group of business owners in the direct selling industry who allowed me to tap into their powerful networks. Also my wife Jeanne vowed to pick up the pieces in our life which I needed her to do that allowed me to focus on my dream. I am also blessed with a tremendous gift of concentration that allows me to compartmentalize numerous projects at a time and focus – focus – focus."

Pressure to Change

"The dream of becoming financially independent and living on the water drove the pressure. When Jeanne became pregnant with our first child, she was put on early bed rest and stopped working outside the home. We had a choice to make of either cutting our lifestyle back or me beginning to generate more income. I was already writing books and speaking but that wasn't getting us to the next level. Once that yacht went by combined with the reality of my deteriorating eyesight, the pressure was on and totally self-inflicted."

Actionable First Steps

"First, I completely changed my attitude towards making money. The reality was that working harder at my job was not getting me ahead so I stopped looking to the University for rewards. I began to build all the equity possible and built avenues of residual income versus trading time for money. My writing focus changed towards generating wealth instead of how to be more effective in an organization. I also let it be known that I was available to speak at almost anytime."

Outcomes of the Change

"Within five years, our family was indeed living on the water. We owned a large portfolio of investment property and paid off all our debt except the home mortgage. I was paddling a kayak to work and bought a car and hired a driver to take me where I needed to go. Most importantly when I was fed up with issues at the University, I was able to retire from teaching and move into a nine-bedroom, five-bathroom house and still live by the water!"

Doug Price and the *Change It!* Model

Problem Recognition

"I was in a career that required me to relocate every few years. That wasn't bad while the kids were young, but I knew this would definitely be a problem later. Climbing the corporate ladder meant more moves and transfers so I had a choice to make. Keep moving the family or choose stability where I make the decisions on staying or moving. I did not want to uproot my family if it was not absolutely necessary. Moving can cause problems for kids in their having to say good-bye to friends and adjust to new schools. Frankly, life is tough enough as it is."

Shared Dream

"After an eighteen-year career with Marriott Hotels, my shared dream was to leave the company on my own accord to start up a business. I shared my dream with my wife Kathy, my mentor Charlie Perkins, and a few other trusted colleagues."

Incentive to Change

"This dream would allow me to take control of both my professional career and family life. Professionally, many people inside of organizations, especially large ones, begin to think about life 'on the outside.' I was no different, especially after six relocations and countless nights away from home attending meetings. I had become totally dependent on a huge company and watched many colleagues lose their jobs, often for cost cutting reasons. I looked in the mirror and knew it could indeed happen to me one day."

Capacity to Change

"Marriott has always enjoyed a fine reputation for its associate training and I was in charge of their hotel sales training programs.

With my background, I felt there was a market for my skill-set that people would have an interest in. Also, for the last seven years with the company, I had primarily functioned as a consultant to the field in a variety of different capacities, including sales training. Personally, my wife Kathy grew up in an entrepreneurial family business environment and was raised in one city, Grand Rapids, MI. She was very accustomed to a family business and really believed in me and encouraged me to try this."

Pressure to Change

"I felt as if I was watching colleagues fall through the holes in the big security net that we all thought was underneath us. Also, I had one "golden handcuff" on already and knew that the longer I stayed, the more difficult it would be to financially leave someday. During my last few weeks at Marriott, I truly felt the company culture was changing. It seemed as if I was constantly getting signs telling me that leaving the company was the right thing to do."

Actionable First Steps

"We incorporated and developed a full business plan along with a corporate identity. We also established a virtual presence online in the final months leading up to my departure from Marriott."

Outcomes of the Change

"In the end, my mentor Charlie Perkins convinced me that I was doing the right thing. After laying out my business plan to him, he smiled and said, 'It sounds great. Just be smart and leave with your head high and don't burn any bridges on the way out. If things don't work out, you can always get a job. And maybe Marriott might become your first client!' As usual, my mentor was exactly right! I learned that in order to save money, my position was not going to be replaced for six months. That turned out to be fortuitous because Marriott did indeed become one of my first clients when they outsourced a large training development project that helped launch my company."

"Business travel now took on a whole new meaning as well. Both my wife and I understood that getting on airplanes generally meant a financial incentive versus simply attending another meeting someplace. That was an important distinction and realization for us."

"I also learned that as a sole entrepreneur, you are often looking for ways to clone or duplicate yourself. You can get so busy working *in your business* that you don't spend enough time working *on your business*. This realization led me to ultimately merge my company with the Miles/LeHane Group which allowed me to spend more time doing what I enjoy doing most: writing, speaking and training."

"Personally, by my leaving the company, we stopped moving our family and raised our kids in the same home for eighteen years. It allowed us to establish roots in a community with schools, teachers, neighbors and church. That 'constant' has been good for all of us, especially our kids. They have friends that they've known their whole lives."

LEARNING FROM THE EXPERIENCE OF OTHERS

We share these personal stories because many adults gain knowledge from other people's stories and experiences. It may come from a family member, co-worker, friend/acquaintance, an author or a perfect stranger. This is not meant to imply that people don't learn in other places. Today, all of us spend time on search engines. But search engines are mainly a source of information, not knowledge. Think about searching for any type of health situation. You can search for symptoms all day long but when it comes to remedies, you trust someone that has first hand experience. To get the knowledge or meaning behind a search, you often need to connect with a real person.

We hope you can relate to our stories. We share them with the hope that it will motivate you to put your own story through the

Change It! Program. It can be revealing, especially when a component is missing!

CHANGE IT! PROGRAM IN A BUSINESS ENVIRONMENT

Now that you have read our personal stories, let us shift gears to a business model. Here is a simple example of the *Change It!* Program using a one time successful restaurant.

Step One: Problem Recognition

A restaurant owner realizes a new competing restaurant is taking customers away and sales are going down.

Step Two: Shared Dream

The owner of the restaurant talks with the entire staff and shares her dream of making the restaurant as successful as it once was.

Step Three: Incentive to Change

The owner wants to stay open for business and be successful once again. She wants to be able to provide good food for her customers as well as maintain her personal lifestyle.

Step Four: Capacity to Change

She has a talented kitchen and service staff along with purveyors supplying the restaurant with good quality products.

Step Five: Pressure to Change

Restaurant sales are down. The owner is having trouble paying invoices on time and is worried about having enough money to make payroll every week.

Step Six: Actionable First Steps

The owner along with the core managers puts together an action plan which includes:

- Shopping all the local competition
- Asking current loyal customers for suggestions
- Asking purveyors for extended credit terms
- Making changes to the menu
- Up-selling contests for the service staff
- E-marketing advertising campaign for their website visitors

With all six of the *Change It!* Program components in place, CHANGE should in fact occur in the restaurant. As you can see, whether the *Change It!* Program is being used for personal or professional reasons, it can work.

Note from Bill and Doug

While all of the parts of the *Change It!* model are important, we think the "Problem Recognition" may be the most useful in understanding why change does, or does not, happen. If you want to change yourself, then you need to know what it is you want to change. If you want to change others, you need to make sure *they* understand that a problem exists. And, we have to say, this is the *problem*! It isn't that people don't understand what the problem is, it is that most people are completely clueless that a problem actually exists.

It doesn't matter if you want to change something small, or something very large and very important. If there is no recognition that a problem exists, nothing will happen. That is why we spend time later in Chapter 8 showing readers how to "stir the pain" in other people. Make them FEEL the pain, and they might just see the problem.

CHAPTER 3

Dig the Well Before You Need the Water

∽

HAVE YOU EVER ASKED YOURSELF:

How did I miss that?

Or:

What was I thinking?

Or:

Why won't this go away?

Problem recognition can be difficult. Let's start to define the difficulty of recognizing a problem with a famous quote: "The average person will not notice a problem until it stands on their toes, smacks them in the face, bites them on the nose, and spits on their head." How is that for a graphic description? It is true, isn't it? Most people are slow to react and in the end, may feel guilty about not recognizing a problem earlier. They need to be totally immersed in a problem before they take action. This chapter is about recognizing a problem before it becomes too annoying.

SCAN THE ENVIRONMENT

When we talk about scanning the environment, we mean the world in which you work, live, and grow. This is your personal environment.

It is proven that all successful businesses have staff members responsible for environmental scanning. Usually, it is a marketing or a strategic planning function. They "look ahead" and make predictions. A company with an effective environmental scanning is seldom surprised by unforeseen events. For the most part, circumstances are predictable.

As we shift to your personal environment, we know that some of our readers are now saying "Are you kidding me? I could not have predicted the car accident that happened to me last year. I was out of work for seven months. How could I have predicted that?"

While it may be impossible to predict specific events, you certainly can make plans for a variety of circumstances. Most families have some sort of trouble in a lifetime. It could be illness, or an accident, or a layoff at work. In other words, you know that *something* is likely to happen. So, don't wait for it to happen before you change. Make some changes *now* so that you will be ready when it happens.

THE REASONABLE MAN THEORY

In the United States, our legal system is based in part on the theoretical actions of the Reasonable Man. In a civil suit, the jury is asked to determine "how a Reasonable Man would have acted in a similar set of circumstances." For example, if a large dog bites a child, the jury is asked "Would a Reasonable Man have foreseen that there was a good chance this dog could bite someone?" The Reasonable Man is expected to look into the future and take positive actions to prevent such a problem.

So we ask you "Would a Reasonable Man understand that there are likely to be some problems in life?" The answer is "Of course he would!" If you could reasonably expect that something bad will happen, doesn't it make sense to make some kind of plan for it? This plan may require you to make some changes now, so that when the unforeseen happens you are prepared.

NO CALAMITY NEEDED

The Reasonable Man doesn't need to prepare for terrible, disastrous events. He (or she, The Reasonable Woman) can simply store up some positive actions today, so that they will pay off in the future. Let us give you a good everyday example.

If you have children, or when you were once a child, you know that situations get more intense as kids get older. When they are young, their relationship with you is pretty simple. You are their whole world! But as they grow, and they start to make friends, they may move away from you. Actually, this is natural, and you want to encourage their independence.

But at the same time they are moving away from your total influence, their lives are getting more complicated. They are subject to more temptations. And, as they become teenagers, their brains may stop working altogether! Can you reasonably predict that this will happen? Of course you can. Even if you have no experience with raising children, you were once a teenager. You know the dumb things you did. You know how confusing and frustrating those times can be.

So the Reasonable Parent works hard to establish good, trusting relationships with children *while they are still young.* Experts agree you have about ten years to build this trusting relationship. Then, when they become teenagers and the unforeseen happens—which was actually perfectly predictable—a strong relationship is hopefully already in place. You can't reconnect with your kids the night they drive a car into the swimming pool! You need to make changes and take action *before* that happens!

Do you want to wait for a crisis before you make changes in your life? Or can you act like a Reasonable Man and make the changes now? If you can do it now, you are "digging the well" before needing the water.

There are many advantages to this. First, you are able to make better decisions before a crisis. Second, if you need to alter your decision, you still have time. Third, and probably most important, you are getting into a great habit. You are taking charge of your life instead of being a victim of circumstances.

DIGGING THEIR WELLS: DOUG AND BILL

To illustrate this concept, think back to both of the authors' *Change It!* stories. We both dug wells before needing the water.

Doug was in a career that required him to relocate every few years. That wasn't bad while his kids were young, but Doug knew that it would definitely be a problem later. He started his own business to have a more stable home for his wife and kids.

Bill wanted financial independence so that he would have more choices as his eyesight deteriorated. Bill is legally blind from Macular Degeneration. However, when circumstances forced Bill to leave his university job, Bill suddenly knew why he had dug his financial well. At age 55, he was able to retire from full-time teaching and pursue a writing and speaking career.

A friend once said he wanted to become bulletproof by creating a financial fortune. He wasn't just talking about money, however. He left his high-pressure, high-risk life as a building contractor to operate a consumer marketing company. He made himself bulletproof in most areas of his life. He had plenty of money, but he also had much more time to spend with family. He used that time to get healthy as well. Today, because he made some changes before a crisis occurred, he has a great lifestyle.

SUCCESSFUL CHANGE MEANS CHANGING FOR SUCCESS

We are going to make some assumptions about why you are reading this book. We will assume that you would like to:

1. Make some changes so you will be more successful

2. Be certain of *what* to change

3. Know *how* to change

4. Help other people to change

In fact, we had to ask ourselves a series of similar questions before we wrote this book. Perhaps the most difficult to ask is why do people want to change? Understanding the "why" is very important.

WHY CHANGE?

Our research told us that many people change only when they are forced into it. Something happens. The circumstances around them change, compelling them to make some sort of adjustment. Some of you readers probably find yourselves in this situation today.

A much smaller number of people look ahead and make adjustments based on their predictions of the future. These are the "dig the well before they need the water" people. You may be reading this book because you are a person like this. If so, congratulations!

But, in either case, whether it is a reaction to a crisis, or a strategy for the future, people want the same thing from any change they make:

1. Avoid problems

2. Achieve success

3. Prevent loss

4. Take advantage of an opportunity

5. Create a positive outcome from any change they make.

WHAT IS SUCCESS?

This raises the question "What is Success?" That isn't the easiest thing to define. In fact, success is very personal. Almost every person has a different definition of what success means. To some people, it is to have a good job, a nice family and a paid-off house. For others, success means flashy cars, dining out at fancy restaurants, and vacations in beautiful resorts. You probably have an idea of what success means to you.

Since each person has a unique view of success, it is hard to say how to achieve success by making strategic changes in your life. We had to come up with an answer to the question "What is success?" in order to give you, our readers, the help you need to succeed.

TRUE SUCCESS

In our humble opinion, you aren't successful unless you have it all! Being wealthy but having no time to enjoy life is not successful. On the other hand, people who have plenty of family time, but not enough money, are not successful either. Success is a balance of all the good things in life.

During seminars, when we ask people to define success, the conversation is often full of controversy and high emotions. Why should our definition of success cause so much anger, panic, and resentment? Because most people have convinced themselves that they are doing okay. Why? Because they look around at the people they know and they say "I am doing okay. Look at my friends. None of them are doing any better."

Sure, in relation to the people you hang out with, you are doing okay. But is that success? Do you have all of the good things—in abundance? Most people try to balance their life at too low a level. In other words, you shouldn't just be looking for balance; you are looking for balance in abundance.

Balance in abundance is a true measure of success. It is when you have it all, in the right proportions. In this book, we are giving you the *Change It!* Program. However, we want you to make the changes necessary to do two things.

1. Have a lot of all the good things (abundance)

2. Have them in the right proportions (balance)

Getting all the good things in life, and having them in the right proportion, is a "dig the well" strategy. It is not a strategy for crisis.

You have to *plan* to have the right things. And you definitely need to plan to have them in the right proportions. It is part of a lifelong strategy of change.

Imagine a life where you have plenty of money. You are not stressed out about finances. Wouldn't that be nice? Now, add good physical, mental and spiritual health. You are happy, confident, content, and aware of the abundance of God's spiritual gifts. Finally, top off that life with strong, loving relationships with family and friends.

That, my friends, is success! If you are missing any of these things, can you really say you are successful?

The Success Barrel

Let us demonstrate this point with an excellent illustration. One of the authors, who was on the Board of Directors of his church, learned about this concept in a church development seminar. It is the barrel concept. We use it here to demonstrate the necessity of *abundance and balance* in achieving success.

Look at the barrel in the drawing below. It is wooden, with staves running vertically from the bottom of the barrel to the top. In this drawing, each of the staves has a name.

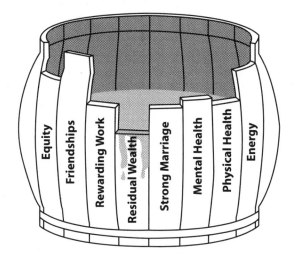

The staves represent all the factors necessary for a successful life. You will see that they have names like "rewarding work," "residual wealth," "strong marriage," "mental health," "physical health," "friendships," and so forth.

Notice that all the staves vary in height. Only one goes all the way to the top of the barrel. The stave marked "residual wealth" is much shorter than the rest. Now, many people would say "Well, this person is still successful, because they have all those other things." But, look at the water that is running out of the barrel. It is pouring over the top of the short stave.

Are you beginning to get the picture? Can you see the problem? It doesn't matter how tall the rest of the staves are! If you have something important missing in your life, or at too low a level, you can't hold success. Consider this:

A barrel only holds water to the level of the lowest stave.

Folks, if you don't have it all, or if you don't have it all in the right proportions, you can't hold water. Your life will "leak" just like the barrel.

Now or Later?

It is up to you. Will you make the changes now while there is still time to think clearly—or later, in mid-crisis? You know things are going to happen. Consider these facts:

1. You do not have financial security. There is no such thing as a safety net anymore. Do you want to live on Social Security? In the next chapter, we examine this area of concern that we call Money.

2. As you get older, you will definitely face health problems. Of course, you could have them at any age. The stress of working 48 hours per week (the average in the U.S.) for an inadequate salary will hurt you both mentally and physically. This area of concern we call Sunny.

3. You cannot establish strong relationships "someday soon." You have to work on them today. Relationships require nurturing and time to grow. Don't wait for a crisis to suddenly discover that you need a better relationship with your spouse, parents, friends or children. This area of concern we call Honey.

Have we got you thinking yet? This is pretty simple stuff. We are offering you the *Change It!* Program. The question is "Will you use it before you desperately need it?"

In this book, we are going to show you how to make changes in three areas—wealth, health and relationships. Let's explore Money, Sunny and Honey in the next chapter.

Note from Bill

I show American parents how to save money on their kids' college education in my business "CollegeSuccessforLess.com." It is amazing to me how many parents know very little about paying for college. It is in all the papers, all the time! Whether it is the cost of tuition or the difficulty getting credit for a student loan, the news is full of dire predictions.

Of course, I have an advantage. I was a college professor for twenty-five years, and I actually *taught* college administrators how to get more money from parents. So, I know the big secrets for saving money. Nonetheless, why do so many parents ignore the huge problem of paying for an education until it is too late?

Here is a real case for "Digging the well before you need the water." Parents need to save money for two reasons. First, they will need fewer loans, and second, it is a great strategy to teach your children! How many lives would change for the better if people just looked ahead, and took some small steps NOW, rather than waiting for a crisis to develop?"

CHAPTER 4

Money, Sunny, and Honey

❦

WHEN WE LOOKED AT ALL THE ATTRIBUTES of a successful person, we were able to put them all into three categories—Money, Sunny and Honey. We mentioned this trio of achievement in the previous chapter, and here we'll explain just what they mean in the context of the *Change It!* Program.

MONEY

Why is everyone so distressed when talking about this subject? This is a question we keep asking ourselves, because everyone we speak to is going crazy about the concept of money!

We can talk about success, goals, dreams, attitudes, relationships, leadership, change, or almost anything else, and these topics don't receive much comment. But the minute we mention the word "money"—especially when we say it is essential for success—people start getting very excited. And they aren't getting excited in a positive way!

Here are just a few examples of the things people say:

"You don't need to have money to be successful."

"Why put Money first? Sunny and Honey are far more important."

"You are always emphasizing money. Don't you feel bad about that?"

"I was always taught that money wasn't the most important thing in life."

And on and on. It happens all the time.

WHAT DO WE MEAN BY MONEY?

Money is just a tool, but it is a very important tool. Remember, we are talking about being *successful* here. We use the word "money" to describe wealth. Having wealth enables you to live a better life. It also enables you to help other people live a better life.

Without money, you are poor. If you are poor, you are not considered successful. Seriously, have you ever seen a poor person and said "Wow, what a success that person is"? Probably not. A person without money is unable to do even the most basic things, like maintain a home, buy food, and so forth. Without money, life is pretty miserable.

There are degrees of money. You can have some money and still not be very successful. If you have great relationships and a fantastic attitude, but you don't have quite enough money to cover emergencies, you will probably find yourself in trouble at some point. Successful people have a fair amount of money.

More importantly, successful people have a *constant, ample supply of money.* They have abundance. You have an abundance of something when you have more than is necessary. You want to have more money than is necessary, because your life can change—quickly.

MONEY AND THE MISSIONARY

One of the authors was at a college reunion recently when a very successful classmate asked about this book. "What is it about?" she asked after hearing the title.

"It is about changing things to achieve success," came the reply.

"How do you define success?" asked the classmate.

"Money, Sunny and Honey!" said the author.

This was immediately followed by the usual set of questions. The most common one of course is "Do people really need money to be successful?" But in the discussion that followed, an interesting new angle came out. The classmate, after reflecting on the explanation, made the following statement:

"We have some friends who are missionaries. They serve people. Surely you aren't saying their lives are not successful?! They are fulfilled. They are admired. They are a success."

The classmate sat back in her chair, certain she had the author trapped. After all, who could trump that one?

But let's look at what missionaries have and what makes them successful. Certainly, they have relationships or Honey. Missionaries, being good people, have the gift of developing relationships. They are committed, enduring, and strong. If a missionary can't form and maintain good relationships, we surely would say they are not successful.

And missionaries probably have good mental, physical and spiritual health or Sunny. For example, would you want to have a missionary around who was unhappy? No. Successful missionaries are positive people. And they need to be healthy in body as well. Their work is hard. If they are not in good health, they are not able to do their missionary field work very well. Certainly, missionaries have a strong spiritual life. Their faith and vision keep them going. Would you want to see a missionary who was weak spiritually? They wouldn't last too long on the mission field, would they?

Successful missionaries do have the last two components—Sunny and Honey. But successful missionaries must also have the first component of successful living—money.

"What?" you are saying. "A rich missionary? Who ever heard of such a thing?"

We will just come out with it: *Successful missionaries need money. Without it, they cannot be successful.*

OUR FAVORITE MISSIONARY

If we gave out "Oscars" for mission work, our award would go to Mother Theresa. What an interesting person she was. She spent a lifetime helping the "poorest of the poor" in Calcutta, India. These people were destitute. She fed them, clothed them, gave them shelter, and most impressively started several hospitals to cure them. She was an inspiration to millions of people around the world.

Mother Theresa also gave spiritual aid to her beneficiaries. But, she didn't just tell them how to live a more spiritual life; she was an example to all of them, and to all of us.

What was the most important task that Mother Theresa performed? She raised money to help her charitable causes. She was a master at creating successful networks of donors. She had money. Of course, she didn't use the money for herself. She didn't hide it in a bank or spend it on big cars. But she was successful because she had Money and Sunny and Honey – all three gifts!

If Mother Theresa did not have money, she would have been just one more poor person in Calcutta. That would have added to the problems, not helped people.

THERE IS NOTHING WRONG WITH MONEY

Are you beginning to feel more relaxed about the subject of money? Folks, you need it! You need to have an abundance of it. Money is important—not in itself—but without money, you cannot be very successful.

In the United States, we are raised with so many bad images of money. Many of the stories we read as children contain moral messages about the evils of money. How many stories did you come across where the villain was a greedy, rich person? Or how many stories do you hear about lottery winners who squander away all their winnings? Some do for sure, and the media reports their trials and tribulations. It is no wonder that we have such a cynical view of money—and the people who have it.

Please, just get over your crazy notions that are holding you back. Money isn't the root of evil. The *love* of money is at the root of evil. We think money is good, because it can be used to do so much good.

Don't be held back by fairy tales. Use your instincts. There is absolutely no reason why you should not have money. You need it. And without money, you are not very successful.

How much money do you need? You need a lot of money to be successful—and, more importantly, it needs to keep coming in whether you work for it or not. You want to create streams of income that are residual. Otherwise, you spend your whole life working, and this is not a successful way to live.

For more information on creating residual income, read Bill Quain's book *Overcoming Time Poverty*. Bill shows you how to create equity that continues to produce income whether you are working or not.

SUNNY

Here is a big part of any successful life—becoming fit and strong in mind, body and soul. We use the word "sunny" to denote a person with a positive outlook on life—a sunny attitude. It comes from improving three types of health—physical, mental and spiritual health.

Of course, the minute we list the three types of health, someone is going to say "Aren't you putting them in the wrong order?" If you are that type of person, go back and read the section on money again. We aren't saying that everyone needs to be an athlete with "six pack abs" and "buns of steel." We are, however, stressing the importance of physical health by placing it first.

PHYSICAL HEALTH

We put physical health first because normally, it is the easiest to change! This is a book called *Change It!* To start making changes, you need to get yourself healthy!

Here are some things to consider about your physical health if you want to be successful.

Weight control – Obesity is a growing problem in the civilized world. It is also a sign that you are not leading the most successful life possible. Obesity means you are well above your normal weight, with a body mass index of 30 or more. Obesity can be caused by overeating and not exercising enough. Get this under control.

Exercise – Everyone can exercise. The problem is many people just don't have the time. They run from one thing to the next. Is this a sign of success? No, it is a sign of overwork! Put down the TV remote and get off the sofa! No matter what your condition is, you can always improve your physical health by doing *some* kind of exercise. In parking lots, park far away from the entrance and walk. Take the stairs instead of escalators or elevators. One of the authors, Bill Quain, is visually handicapped, yet he has discovered many ways to keep in shape. For six years, Bill *kayaked* to work in Miami. He turned his challenge—not driving a car—into a great exercise routine.

Smoking – If you are addicted to tobacco, you are not successful. Why? Because it will make you sick and you will die too soon. Think of all the methods to stop smoking from acupuncture to will power and everything in-between. This is a real *"Change It!"* situation.

Alcohol – We have no problems with the moderate consumption of alcohol. In fact, studies indicate that moderate amounts may have positive effects on the heart. But, alcohol addiction is an increasing problem. We have friends who are alcoholics and they are unsuccessful. We also have friends who are recovering alcoholics. They overcame their addictions and created positive, successful lifestyles. If alcohol is a problem for you, avoid it and seek help.

Drugs – Illegal drugs are one thing. You know about those dangers. But prescription drugs can also be a huge problem for your physical health. Be careful not to mix prescription drugs and don't become dependant on them.

Your physical condition is important to your success. Go join a health club or a local pool. Sign up for an exercise class. Walk daily with your spouse or a neighbor. Sign up for a charity walk or run. If you are not living a positive lifestyle—*Change It!*

MENTAL HEALTH

Like physical health, you might have some limitations in the mental area. You could have an underlying chemical imbalance. That's okay; you can still *maximize* your mental health.

Here are some areas to work on:

Stress – If you are stressed out, it is probably because you are not successful in some area. For example, if you don't have enough money, it causes stress. Stress kills—you and your relationships.

Anger – You have a choice with anger—just like most situations. *You* are the one who is angry. It is a choice. You are letting something make you angry. Stop giving people and situations power over your emotions.

Motivation – Successful people are motivated by their own success. If you just don't seem to have the energy to get things done, you need to set your dreams and get going. Look for small accomplishments first and then build from there.

Sleep – Disorders such as insomnia, sleep apnea, and narcolepsy are serious conditions that can be treated by professionals to help your overall mental health. But there are also simple sleep problems—even just not getting enough! *Change It!*

These are just a few of the attitudes and conditions that mark a healthy or unhealthy mental condition. For the most part, you have control over them. You can decide to be happy or you can allow yourself to be sad. Motivation and commitment come directly from you. Perseverance is a mark of the successful person.

Without good mental health, you are unsuccessful. If you need special help, get it. Since this book is about change our advice to improve one aspect of mental health is to think about this. We believe it is easier and quicker to change the way you *react* to people (and situations) than it is to *change others.*

SPIRITUAL HEALTH

The third part of "Sunny" is your spiritual health. This is a critical area for your success. We aren't talking about going to church here. We are talking about a sense of living for a greater good. Yes, you may find this in church. But we believe *you are the church always and everywhere you go.* It is much more than simply going to church once a week. We feel successful people create, and build, spiritual health by consistently demonstrating their "sunny."

Here are some things to consider.

- **Look for the good in others** – Successful people recognize the beauty of others. Don't look for the imperfections.

- **Give your time** – Help others by giving time. This is your most precious gift.

- **Give your money** – Support a missionary family with money and prayer or give to a local charity.

- **Give your energy** – Become an energizer. This is one of the greatest traits of the successful person. Light up the room when you walk in. This lifts up others.

The best way to improve your spiritual health is to help others to grow and change. Look for the opportunity—every single day—to help others. You will be amazed at how you will grow and what a humbling feeling it can be.

HONEY

Relationships are the currency of life, and successful people have successful relationships! What makes their relationships work? Everyone has a different set of solutions. However, this does bring up a point that many people make about relationships; "What ever works, works." If a relationship is going fine, don't overanalyze it! Just do not take it for granted and enjoy it.

On the other hand, here are some things that make good relationships:

Trust – Is there anything more important? We don't think so. In a good relationship, *both* parties must be able to completely trust each other. Once trust is broken, it is possible but difficult to re-engage. There is a simple rule for gaining someone's trust—be trustworthy. Just look at the word "trustworthy." Are you? Do you do things that are consistently worthy of the trust of another human being? Trust is important in both business and personal relationships. Do a "Trust Audit" of your relationships. Don't expect others to get trustworthy until you are. A recommended resource in this area is the book, *The Speed of Trust* by Stephen M.R. Covey.

Truth – This is a tricky one. For example, is it a good idea to give a truthful answer to the question "Does this dress make me look fat?" We think not. However, there is no substitute for the truth in most situations. As Mark Twain said "If you always tell the truth, you don't have to remember what you said."

Consistency – Now, we should point out that being consistently *bad* is not what you want. However, don't miss this point. Being able to depend on a consistently upbeat attitude, kind behavior, and a total commitment to a relationship is important. Are you consistent or moody?

Have you ever worked for someone who was not consistent? You know the type of person we mean. When you go into the office each day, the first question everyone asks is "Is she in a good mood today?"

What a terrible way to conduct a relationship. Consistency is closely related to trust.

Giving – You have to bring something to the relationship. It may be a sense of humor, knowledge (especially in business), warmth, and do forth. One-sided relationships don't last.

We have all been in relationships at both work and home that are one-sided. These just aren't healthy. If both people "give" the result will be greater than what either put in. Think of it as a tennis match—serve *and* volley.

Commitment – In order for a relationship to grow, it must have time. Again, this is true for both business and personal relationships. You can only have time to grow if both parties are committed to a long-term relationship.

In a committed relationship, people can get over small hurts and inconsistencies provided there is open communication. Strong bonds need time to develop.

HOW HONEY CREATES SUCCESS

Which came first, the successful relationship or the successful person? It is difficult to separate the two situations. You can't be a success without strong relationships (Honey) and you can't have a successful relationship if you don't exhibit the behaviors of a good person. So, in our opinion, it is the *process* of working on your relationships that makes you successful.

Who do you know that has successful relationships? What kind of person are they? Are they suspicious and secretive or are they open and friendly?

Building strong relationships, both at work and at home, is a full-time job. Like we said with "sunny", it is a continual gift. As we talk more about the *Change It!* Program you will observe the importance of relationships. And, you will discover their great secret.

THE GREAT SECRET OF RELATIONSHIPS

This is the big secret: People are selfish. They do things that bring them rewards. They won't do things that don't bring rewards.

Yes, that is the big secret, and it is certainly the big secret in relationships. If you want someone to stay committed to a relationship, you have to make sure they get more out of the relationship than they put in. You have to make sure they fulfill their selfish motives. It's really about putting someone's wants and needs before your own.

We've all been taught that it is bad to be selfish. But, the truth is, we are all selfish people. We do things best when they give us what we want.

It is okay! We would much rather be in a positive relationship with a person who is getting what they want out of it than with someone who is constantly putting in more than they receive. We give them what they want so they will keep coming back for more.

We might contrast selfish behavior with unselfish behavior. An altruistic person is someone who does good deeds for an unselfish reason. For example, earlier, we talked about Mother Theresa, the famous missionary. She was certainly altruistic.

How many Mother Theresas do you know? Have you ever worked with one? Yes, there are some people (let's say one in a million) who function well in an altruistic lifestyle. None of them ever worked for us—and, we've had many employees between us!

Being in a relationship with a regular person can be a great thing. But regular people have regular motivations. They want something. They are selfish.

We have to work at getting over this idea that being selfish—that is we do things because it gives us what we want—is wrong. Being *greedy* is wrong. Expecting something for nothing is wrong. Cheating people by lying to them is wrong. But doing things because you get a reward is okay!

An example of "it is okay to be selfish" took place during a faculty meeting at a Florida university. The professors of a certain department were talking about the need to get more work done. The Dean said, "We need some people to volunteer to work extra for the good of the school."

Nobody spoke up. Everyone just sat there, waiting for the meeting to proceed so they could all go home.

One brave professor spoke up. "Why not offer some kind of reward to the people who do the extra work?" he asked. The Dean was not happy. He wanted volunteers, not a discussion of rewards.

Then, another professor spoke up. "Someone should volunteer. It is for the good of the school. Whatever happened to altruism?"

Nobody had an answer to that question. And nobody volunteered. The matter was dropped and no action was taken.

The administrator at that school made the mistake that many, many people make when trying to establish relationships. He didn't recognize a simple truth. People respond to selfish impulses. Nothing wrong with that—unless you don't remember it!

BUILD WITH SELFISH REWARDS

Build relationships, and get things accomplished, by understanding that people respond to selfish impulses. Learn to *give* to a relationship. This satisfies the selfish needs of the other person. Then, you will *receive* from the relationship and benefit by achieving your selfish ambitions.

By now, you probably think we are pretty crazy, if not downright cynical. You can believe what you want, but this stuff works. And remember, this is a book called *"Change It!"* You are reading this book because you want to change something, right?

Change your assumptions about people. Build relationships with incentives and you will get what you want. Relationships only grow and remain strong if there is a reward for each person. Does a parents' love diminish over the years if the child is bad? Maybe not. But, the parent cannot keep on giving without a return. The same is true of a spouse. It is *certainly* true of a friend, or a business partner!

Build your relationships—all of them—by giving. Give respect, knowledge, love, trust, companionship—whatever the other person really wants from the relationship. This applies to all relationships. Give to get.

To build a relationship, you must give. To maintain a relationship, you must get back! Choose your life partners carefully. Use your head, because these are the biggest decisions you make in this life. If a relationship isn't working out in the beginning, don't assume that more giving on your part will change it. You can go "emotionally broke" in a bad relationship.

Choose your relationship partners like you would hire an employee. Interview them. Observe them. Get references. You can avoid many problems by refusing to hire a bad employee. You can make a huge difference in your life by avoiding a bad relationship before it evolves.

RECAP: THREE AREAS OF SUCCESS

We define success as having an ample supply of money; having good physical, mental, and spiritual health; and having strong relationship with the people in your life. Money, Sunny, Honey. We hope that understanding this broad and detailed definition of success will help you look at your own life and make decisions about just how you need to *Change It!*

Note from Bill and Doug

How can we talk about change if we don't define the life conditions we want to change to? While each of us may define success differently, it is important to remember that everyone wants success. So, we can use it to help generate Problem Recognition, and we can especially use it for the Shared Dream portion of *Change It!* Program.

Success is not a subtle word. It is very bold, very blatant. It doesn't come easily, and can be fleeting without constant work. But, nothing worthwhile comes easy. We would like to encourage our readers, and remind you that the hard work is worth it if we achieve true success—Money, Sunny and Honey—in abundance.

Prioritize

THIS CHAPTER CAN SAVE YOU and the people around you a great deal of grief. We will show you how to choose the particular areas to change and how to avoid changing everything else.

First of all, some things aren't worth the effort. Mark Twain observed, "Don't try to teach a pig to sing. It wastes time and annoys the pig." That saying applies here. Don't waste your time trying to change people who don't want to change, or who won't benefit from the change. And don't waste time on things that don't make your life better.

We know we sound a little hard-hearted here. But your time is very precious. And you can only do so much. If you become known as a person who is *always* changing things—for no apparent reason—you will quickly run out of people to work with.

A SIMPLE RULE

We just spent a lot of our book time telling you about success. Success is measured in terms of three gifts—Money, Sunny and Honey. Here is our simple rule for you:

If it doesn't increase your success, don't do it!

Is that simple enough? If you are not going to get more Money, Sunny or Honey, don't get involved. You are wasting your time. Whatever it is, your involvement will only be misdirected because it will take away from your success.

For example, let's say you manage a sales team. On that team, there are six people. Two of them are superstars, bringing in more than 60% of the revenues. But, those two salespeople are not filling out their "Sales Contact Sheets" correctly. This neglect of paperwork is in direct contradiction to company policy.

One of the other salespeople (the least productive, of course) complains that he is spending time filling out the contact reports and this is why he isn't as productive. He wants you to "make some changes around here so that everyone—no exception—fills out those reports." You agree, because it is really annoying that those two super salespeople are not doing *exactly* what you told them to do.

Don't do it! What do you possibly have to gain by annoying your top producers? Will you make more money? Will this improve your superstars' mental, physical or spiritual health? And how about your relationships? If you align yourself with the weakest member of the team, you are bound to stir up trouble in the relationship department.

However, if you *must* change something here, look for the things that have a positive impact. Look for the things that improve Money, Sunny and Honey. Here are a couple of changes you might make.

1. Fire the weakest person—not because he complained, but because he used the Sales Contact Sheet as an excuse. You don't need this distraction.

2. Change the system for filling out the Sales Contact Sheet to make it easier for the top people. Here is a thought— buy them digital voice recorders and ask them to simply record all their contacts. Then, have an assistant type up all the information. If you require names and addresses, let the assistant compile that information. Just get the absolute, minimum from those top salespeople. Keep them productive—especially if it helps you make your quota. The more time people spend doing what they do best—the more productive and happy they will be!

3. Turn the paperwork problem into a reward by showing the less productive salespeople that you will take over some of their "drudge" work if they make improvements in their

sales figures. (They won't, because this wasn't the real problem anyway!) But it will give you some peace of mind because you can say "Well, if you prioritized your efforts and produced more, I would make your life easier. But, right now, you are making my life more difficult, so I am not inclined to ease up on you."

Whatever you do, don't get involved in negative thinking with negative people. It can only be bad.

KEEP THE MISSION IN MIND

Remember, you are on a mission. You want to create more Money, more Sunny, and more Honey in your life. That is it, pure and simple. That is your mission.

All we are saying is to do the things that bring success, and don't do anything else. There are so many people out there who want to get you off track. Read about "Time Bandits" and "Black Holes" in Bill's book *Overcoming Time Poverty*.

In the book *Every Man a Tiger*, General Chuck Horner said "The name of the game is to complete the mission." He spoke about the different *tactics* he tried, but he never deviated from the overall mission—to succeed. While the mission you are on may not be as intense as fighting a war, it is, nonetheless, your mission. And, like everyone else, your mission is to succeed.

Don't forget that, and don't get sidetracked. We can't stress this enough. If you keep your eye on the mission, and if you really *understand* the goals of your mission, it becomes easier to stay on track. The changes you need to make become clear.

People are depending on you. If you work in an organization, they depend on you. If you supervise others, they certainly depend on you. If you have a family, well—you get the picture. The man or woman who knows what they want to achieve is dependable and strong. He or she has the best interests of everyone around them in mind.

In The Real World

Yes, we know. You work and live in the real world. It is sometimes difficult to focus purely on the mission because of all the distractions—the politics and game-playing that goes on in every organization and in every situation. Perhaps you want us to write something here like:

"Don't worry, we understand. You have to make allowances for all the other stuff in your life and business. You need to play the game! Just do your best, and it will be okay."

Sorry, this is a chapter about setting priorities. And this is a book about changing things so you will be successful—not so you can hug everybody and live in harmony. There are plenty of "feel good" books out there, and this isn't that kind of book. This is a *feel better* book!

Folks, so many people think the "real world" is made up of confusing situations that must be finessed with compromises. To a certain extent, we suppose this is true. You do need to be situationally aware.

But we are talking about *change* here. If you find yourself in an impossible situation, and if you can't change the situation, you have to change your position! If you can't succeed, *Change It!* That is a change worth making.

Success is Hard

If you attain success, under the terms we describe, you will have a fantastic life! How many people do you know who actually have a fantastic life? Do you know *anyone at all* who can truthfully say "I have it all." We don't know too many.

No, most of the people we know keep saying the same old things again and again. They either tell us how they gave up money (or therefore, increased their stress levels any time they had an unexpected expense) to spend more time with family and friends. Or, they tell us how they are working so many hours because they are creating a great lifestyle for their families.

These are not successful people! They are semi-successful.

If you are way down on the success spectrum right now, it is fine to set some interim goals. It is acceptable to start working your way out of a hole. For example, if you do not have enough money, we don't expect you to overcome that problem right away. If you have been ignoring your physical, mental and spiritual health for decades, you can't expect to gain it all back on a weekend of exercise, psychiatry, and church-going.

If you start making changes to just "make things a little better" you will never get anywhere worthwhile. Set your goals high. Set your priorities. Be realistic with the timetable of your expectations but never forget the mission.

BE FLEXIBLE

At this point, some readers are undoubtedly banging your fists on the desk and shouting "I knew it. I need to be tough—to set the direction and give some orders. We need to get this thing accomplished."

We know that some of you are doing this because we are, to some degree, control freaks as well. But, this isn't our point at all. You have to be smart about this. You need to understand that not everyone will *share* your vision—especially as it pertains to your personal success. The fact that you want to be successful will be completely uninteresting to almost everyone else.

Here is what you do. Set the big goal and the mission. Make any big changes you need, and then make small course corrections as the situation dictates. Don't simply make a decision then put it on autopilot.

After a presentation to a large group, author Bill Quain had the opportunity to speak to some of the group's leaders. One man had been a scientist at NASA for many years. He told Bill about course corrections on rocket ships.

"When we send a rocket on a long journey," said the scientist, "everyone knows the ultimate goal. For example, it may be to get some surface craft on Mars. Everyone is doing their part to make the mission—getting to Mars—a success. We launch the rocket, and it is *aimed* at Mars."

"However, we can't possibly expect a rocket, traveling millions of miles, to actually hit the target. And, to complicate matters even more, if it is off just a little bit as it leaves earth, it will be way *off* by the time it reaches Mars. So, we put two small rockets on board to make very small course corrections every day. These small corrections make it possible to avoid *major* corrections later. We accomplish the mission by keeping our eyes on the target, even though it is far off. We need to make course corrections a priority or the mission fails."

ONCE YOU LAUNCH THE ROCKET

That NASA example is a fantastic metaphor for your life. You need to pick a target, launch your rocket, and then make the constant adjustments necessary to keep on course. Otherwise, you will end up in outer space, out of oxygen, and all alone! (Okay, it won't be that bad! You can always depend on the government or your children to take care of you. Frankly, we don't trust either one to keep us in comfort!)

Imagine if those space engineers launched the rocket, then got distracted by some other things? Suppose the chief engineer decided that a committee meeting was more important than calculating course corrections. By the time he got back from the meeting, and writing up the fifteen page report that pointed out how much better he was performing than the other engineers, the spacecraft could be hopelessly off course. The effort to bring it back would be too much.

Or, what if the chief engineer decided that it was too much trouble to keep the rocket pointed at Mars. Would the mission be fulfilled if he said, "You know, we are really closer to Venus. Let's just head there and call it a success."

Finally, what if he came up with some kind of excuse like, "We could have sent the rocket to Mars, but then we would have to work too hard. So, we sent it to Cincinnati and we all went bowling."

Folks, make the big changes necessary to get your personal or business rocket on target *in the beginning of the project*. Then, *prioritize* everything in your life to keep your dreams on track! Make the small changes as necessary—be flexible. You may go way off course if you do not keep your hands on the joystick.

Note from Bill and Doug

This is a powerful chapter, with lots of good ideas and strategies. However, our favorite gem is a small quote that may have gone unnoticed by our readers. We tell people that this is not a *feel good book*, it is a *feel better book*. We are very serious about helping our readers create a better life—one filled with an abundance of Money, Sunny and Honey. We don't want them to feel good about where they are now. We want them to feel uncomfortable about where they are now.

This is a big difference between our book and some others we read. But, we look at it this way—if things were so good now, why did you buy a book on change?!

Do the same thing for other people that we are doing for you. Help them find Problem Recognition, then help them prioritize. Don't do things that take you away from your *personal* mission. Don't be distracted. Share the Dream and get others focused as well.

∾ Part II - Changing People

In Part I, you learned about changing yourself. This is a difficult and daunting task. But, it is nothing compared to the task of changing others! This is impossible—unless you know some fundamental secrets and strategies.

In the special "Read This First" portion of this book, we showed you that Change is Choice, and then Change is *your* choice. We also told you that, if you work with other people (and who doesn't?) you needed to make Change *their* Choice. That's what we cover in this section.

If you want others to change, they must want the change. You do this by putting them into the *Change It!* Model, starting with Problem Recognition, and working through to Actionable First Steps. But, in this section, you will learn about the most important part of working with others— creating *internal* pressure that motivates them to change. By doing this, you make Change *their* Choice.

CHAPTER 6

Mission Impossible—
Ego Check

⌒

WE HAVE SOME GOOD NEWS and some bad news for you. First, the good news. You will be able to have an impact on many people in getting them to change. Now, the bad news. It doesn't always work! There are some people you can *never* get to change, and, there is even *worse* news. *Nobody* will change every time or exactly when you want them to.

We want you to have a realistic set of expectations. Unless you are a hypnotist, you simply can't exert enough pressure to get everyone to do what you think they should do when you want them to do it. Some people will never recognize problems or when they do, they simply give it tacit approval.

FAKING IT

We just gave a seminar on change to a group of managers. We showed them how to use the *Change It!* Program to Recognize the Problem, Share the Dream, and so forth. After a while, one of the younger managers said "I am paid to be a leader. A leader leads. Why do I need to go through all of this? If I am the manager, aren't I paid to decide what should be done? Then, if I am a good leader, shouldn't I just be able to tell my people what to do and expect them to do it? If I want to change the way we do something, I should be able to skip all this stuff and just change it."

To professional speakers and trainers, a moment like this is known as a "reality check." This young man was obviously struggling with the information, trying to figure out why he couldn't just command change and have it be done. In fact, for some insignificant change, this may be sufficient. But, for really meaningful change, on a deep level, it is absolutely the wrong thing to do.

Why? Because people will *Fake It*! They may *look* like they are thinking and acting differently, but inside, where it counts, they are thinking "Okay, this will go away soon. Then we can get back to doing things the old way."

When we talk about getting other people to change, we aren't just talking about some surface actions. We are talking about *a relatively permanent shift* in things like attitude, heart, beliefs, and so forth. Meaningful change requires a meaningful investment of time and energy.

Any parent knows what we are talking about. Your kids will *look* like they are doing what you suggest, at least in front of you. But every parent knows that their kids are capable of some pretty two-faced actions! Parents *should* know this for one, very good reason—we did the same things when we were kids.

Faking change is very common in organizations. Good leaders recognize it is sometimes much easier to fake it rather than have real change. Mediocre leaders do some pretending themselves—faking the fact that they know the employees are faking. Bad leaders never catch on. They keep saying things like, "My people do exactly what I ask them to do."

WHO CAN YOU CHANGE?

We don't mean to imply that creating change is only appropriate for the workforce. Yes, it is sometimes easier to slip into this "corporate mindset." People are always talking about their workplace. One of the things people talk about the most is change: how they would change things if they were in charge, how the boss wants them to change, and they ask that question, "Why can't those people I work with just change and get it right?"

We inevitably talk about organizational change when we discuss the subject. But, you can help change many types of people: your kids, your spouse (be careful with this one!) friends, associates, and so forth.

BECOMING A CHANGE AGENT

In order to help others to change, begin with "checking your ego at the door." You are not a master of change, you are a change agent. An agent is someone who acts as a go-between. An agent *represents* others. Think of famous entertainment and sports personalities. They all have agents. Most of us can name the famous personality, but few of us know the names of their agents.

An agent of change is working for the good of the people who will change. This is an act of service, not a command. To be a true agent, you must put the good of the people you change above your own. This is why we say your ego needs to be out of the process.

What do we mean? Let's take a few examples.

1. You are in business for yourself, and you want to make money by helping other people start a business in your line. Direct Selling programs are a classic example. To do this, you need to help those other people see that they have a problem. Usually, the problem is that they do not have enough money to do the things they want. To be successful in this business, you must decide to be in a new type of business. In his book *B2B Means Back to Basics*, Bill Quain calls this "Being in the business of building business builders."

2. You are the manager of a medium-size business. Your business is making money, but it could be doing much better. You help your employees make changes so that the *employees* will do better—make more money, participate in

profit sharing, have an easier day at work, and get home on time to see their families.

3. You have a teenage child who is a sophomore in high school. She is not paying attention to her homework and test scores. You work to help change her attitudes, and ultimately her actions. The whole purpose of the exercise is so that she will have more good choices later in her life.

4. You are the coach of a soccer team. Your players need to get more practice so they can win more games. You discover that you are unable to help them technically with their play-running strategies, so you bring in an outside expert to coach them before the next big game.

In all these cases, you are the agent for change. You want the change so that others can become successful. Sure, you want the success yourself, but you get what you want by helping others get what they want.

Let's contrast this with the young man who said "I am the leader..." during the seminar we gave. He wanted to be in control, to be in charge. If there was going to be change, he wanted it to be *his* change. He wanted to know if he could skip all the *Change It!* steps and just tell people what they needed to do.

The idea of authority is a big problem for many people. They want to be in charge, to create a company, or an association board of directors, or a family, in their own image. That is big time ego! They want to decide on the changes and then make sure everyone pulls their weight.

In the very first part of this book, we said that we would teach you how to attain three things—Money, Sunny and Honey. Throughout the book, we remind you that we are aiming pretty high. We aren't going to go to all the trouble of writing a book just so you could be a *little better* at work. We don't want to spend all this time just so you could get your kid to mow the lawn. We are dealing in big, meaningful, relatively permanent changes that affect the lives of many other people.

If you want those big things, you have to make some big adjustments yourself. One of those adjustments is to give up your ego. Sorry, but this isn't about you! You are in it for others. Yes, you may benefit, but if you really want to make an impact, take your eyes off yourself and gaze upon on others.

This means to aspire and become a *servant* leader. You need to do everything you can so that others can succeed. You need to intervene in their lives so they see the problem and then come to you for help to resolve it.

This means, as a change agent, you do the hard work. You are the one with the dream. Now, you have to share it with others. But, remember, they don't want your dream. They want their own dream. Help them find it and then help them achieve it.

WHO IS THE EASIEST TO CHANGE?

The answer to this question might surprise you. If you have people you would like to help change, don't look for the most self-contented person. Don't look for the happiest person. They are less likely to change than the slightly unhappy person.

If someone is totally happy, totally satisfied with their life, they have no reason to change. If they have everything they want, why would they place it all in jeopardy? See Step One of the *Change It!* Program.

You are looking for the person with a slight bit of dissatisfaction. This is the person who will *act* to make things better. They are the people who can see, that with a little effort, they could have much more. To them, the prospect of change is not as scary as it is to the person who is *very unhappy*, or the person who is *very happy*.

Sometimes, we can get so confused and misled by the simplest things. Bill Quain was giving a workshop from his program *College Success for Less* recently. Bill was talking about getting college loans. Bill's advice: "Shop around. Get the loan with the lowest total payback possible."

One person in the audience said, "Shouldn't we only borrow money from banks we trust?"

Bill's answer was emphatic. "No! You don't care who you *borrow* money from. You only care who you *lend* money to! Why should you care if the company that lends you money goes out of business? You *want* them to go out of business. Then you may not have to pay back the loan!"

The same theory applies to slightly unhappy changers, versus totally happy non-changers. We want our people, our family, and our employees to be happy and content. Yet, when it comes time to get them going on a worthwhile plan of change, we should be looking for the slightly unhappy people.

In attempting to read people, it is important to observe various personality types. Let's take a look at the simple system below. Later in Chapter 11, we will remind you of these personality types as your communication targets.

FOUR PERSONALITY TYPES

There are many systems out there that divide personalities into four types. However, the one we like the most is probably the oldest of the systems. In fact, even after searching on the internet, we are unable to discover who came up with this system. We know it was in use in the 70's. But, we just can't figure out who first delivered it. So, with our apologies to the author, we will show it to you here.

In this system, the four personalities are on an x, y grid. The vertical axis represents the degree of assertiveness (top half of grid) and passivity (lower half of grid.) The horizontal arrow represents the degree of task orientation (left side) or people orientation (right side). The grid's four quarters are named:

Top left quadrant – Controllers

Bottom left side – Analyzers

Top right side – Promoters

Bottom right side – Supporters

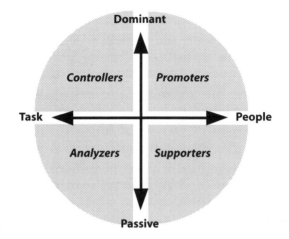

A Controller is someone who is assertive, and task-oriented, while an Analyzer is task oriented and passive. Conversely, the Promoters are assertive and people oriented, while the Supporters are people oriented and passive.

Each of these basic personality types has an ingrained belief system. Certain things make sense to them, and other things do not. Or, if "making sense" is too strong a phrase, try this: each personality type will feel more comfortable with information that is presented in a certain way. And, since they are more likely to respond favorably to certain kinds of message delivery, they are more likely to believe those messages.

You can imagine how important this is in selling an idea like a *Change It!* strategy. If your prospects are more likely to believe a message that is delivered in a certain way, then doesn't it make sense to deliver it that way?

Here are some general strategies for each personality type:

Controllers – They want to be in charge, and they want it done their way. So let them discover the message on their own. Help them come to conclusions, but never deliver the message to them as "your idea."

Promoters – They never met an idea they didn't like! These are creative people. They don't mind hearing the basics of the message, but they want to add their own twists. Let them take your message further.

Analyzers – They like to "weigh" the pros and cons of a situation. Give them facts—all the facts. Don't hurry them, or push them. If the idea is a good one, and you have given them all the information they need, they can be your biggest friends.

Supporters – Make sure they see the human element here. Show them how everyone will feel better. They want to believe you, and in you.

Note from Bill and Doug

Our favorite part of this chapter is telling people to look for the slightly discontent person when it comes to finding a *Change It!* target. These are the people you are looking for. Why? Because they are looking for you! Slightly discontent people are usually pretty capable, but they have some sort of problem. They might be a little unsure of what the problem is exactly. This is where you come in, with Problem Recognition. Stir the pain! Help them see the problem, then help them share in the dream.

Changing Circumstances

ᕙᕗ

THERE ARE TWO WAYS TO HELP other people change. You can get them into the *Change It!* Program by giving them problem recognition, or you can change their circumstances. In previous chapters, we have talked about the importance of problem recognition and the fact that in its absence there is no chance for change. In this chapter, we will focus more on changing their circumstances.

Why is this even important? The truth is, changing a set of circumstances is often much easier than changing people's minds, hearts, and attitudes. By simply changing the circumstances, you can get them to change their actions. They don't have to do a full buy-in. They may not even realize it is happening!

STARBUCKS COFFEE

Here is a great example of what we are talking about. In 2008, Starbucks Coffee Company made a radical change to help the culture of their company—and hopefully, their falling stock price. They closed each and every one of their stores for three hours to "retrain their employees and to make significant changes in their image."

We can use Starbucks three-hour closing as an example of putting people into the *Change It!* Program. But a visit to the franchise revealed a smaller procedural change as well.

When we ordered our coffees, the counterperson asked us each for our first names, and then wrote them on our respective cups. This was a change in procedures. Before, the Starbucks employee would write down all the special directions for the cup of coffee. For example, Bill ordered a grande skinny decaf latte. (Most of you know what that is.) One week later at the same Starbucks, after the young woman made the necessary notations on the cup, she asked Bill for his name. She wrote that on the cup too.

Why the change? If you have ever been at a Starbucks when it is busy, you would understand. There is always a group of people waiting for their various coffees at the end of the line. It is confusing when the young lady announces *"Who has the double moccachino, venti, all-beef, Kosher, latte and milkshake combo?"* Okay, that is an exaggeration. But how many times do people grab the wrong coffee, setting off a chain reaction of unhappy customers?

Here is something to remember about customers—no matter what business you are in. Customers are not paying attention! They are thinking about other things. They are on their cell phones, or arguing with someone, or making plans for the weekend. They are doing everything but paying attention to their coffee order.

Starbucks had a problem, and they had a choice. They could have spent a great deal of time trying to get their customers into the *Change It!* Program, then train their customers to pay attention, or they could simply change the circumstance. They went for the simpler and much more effective solution—change the circumstance.

While most people can't remember the type of coffee they order, quite a few of them can remember their names—unless it is their first cup of coffee in the morning! So while hearing a string of complicated, meaningless phrases shouted out might not reach the subconscious of many customers, folks jump to attention and quickly respond to the most important word in any language—their own name. For more information on the power of names from a service standpoint, see Doug Price's book *License to Serve*.

AN IMPERFECT COFFEE WORLD

Unfortunately, the young lady at Starbucks did not call out our names at the other end of the line on our last visit. Our names were written on our cups. She *could* have read them out. Instead, she looked at us and rattled off our order specifications, but not our names. She *should* have said, *"Bill, here is your double moccachino, venti, all-beef, Kosher, latte and milkshake combo. Enjoy it!"*

But this happened only a few days after the short-term closing. We hope, if anyone from Starbucks is reading this right now, that they will begin *using* the names they collect.

THE BGO

A friend of ours refers to these moments as a "Blinding Glimpse of the Obvious," or a BGO. No matter how well you plan, no matter how much you train people, they often miss the point when you change the circumstance. The problem is, they have not had a Problem Recognition, developed a Shared Dream, or any of the other great facets of the *Change It!* Program. Forgetfulness is a challenge with using the change of circumstance approach.

You must be constantly on guard and monitoring the situation. The minute you leave an uncommitted person, they are likely to make some changes of their own.

What could the problem have been at Starbucks that day? Shouldn't it have been obvious to the employees that a major push was on to make new commitments to the customer? After all, what did it cost the company to close for three hours? Forget the missed business on that day. Forget the three hours of pay for no sales. Think about the possible lost customers who needed a coffee and went someplace else.

We must admit, though, as a public relations stunt, the closing was brilliant!

To clearly demonstrate the right way to create change by circumstance, let's talk about a series of five steps you can use to avoid most change circumstance problems.

BEGIN AT THE END

The system we use is called "Backwards Design." It starts at the end, not at the beginning. We decide what *outcome* we want and then work backwards from there to create a set of circumstances that almost forces the person to make the changes, and therefore, reach the desired outcome. This system works with customers, employees, children, spouses, friends, and business acquaintances. It isn't foolproof, but it really helps.

Remember, this system is for people who do not share your dream and who may not see the problem. However, unless they do certain things differently, *your* dream will fade away!

BACKWARDS DESIGN IN THE *CHANGE IT!* PROGRAM

1. *Problem recognition* – This applies to you. If you don't know why a change is needed, you will not go through all the trouble to design the circumstance correctly.

2. *Desired outcome* – What do you want? Specifically, Starbucks wanted a satisfied customer and to make sure that every person got the right coffee. In addition, they wanted to get back to an old practice of using the customers' names.

3. *Increase capacity and decrease choice* – Many changes fail because the change agent does not give the right people the necessary tools, decision making capability, and other resources necessary to carry out changes. On the other hand, you want to limit the choices. Remember, this system is for simple changes.

4. *Create incentives and disincentives* – Here is an easy cure for the Starbucks problem: Give customers a coupon for a free cup of coffee if the person who takes the order and the person who delivers it do not use the customer's name.

Would the employee be more likely to remember to use the name if the customer was going to pounce on the opportunity to get a free cup of coffee? How many free cups would each employee be allowed to give out before being suspended—or worse?

5. *Clearly communicate* – Articulate every aspect of the change, starting with the desired outcome, and ending with the incentives/disincentives. We cannot overstate the importance of this communication. Test it! Evaluate it!

Remember, you are the one with the vision, the problem recognition and the dream. You are working with people who are largely uncommitted to your vision of the future. They want to be helpful. They have good intentions. However, they do not share your complete understanding of the system, the details and the overall goals.

Who Can You Change This Way?

This system will work with almost anyone who has a dependent relationship with you. It could be customers, employees, children, and so forth. It can also work with spouses and friends, but there are some potential problems there. You want to be seen as manipulating the situation to reach *their* goals, not yours.

However, to show you just how universal this system *can* be, here are some examples of changing circumstance with a spouse, and a child.

Backwards Design Examples

Spouse

1. **Problem recognition:** A spouse realizes that she can help the family financial situation by taking on a part-time home business.

2. **Desired outcome:** Less stress on the family and more money for family expenses.

3. **Increase capacity/Decrease choice:** With a part-time working spouse, there will be duties and chores that have to be divided up among family members. There will also be activities that have to be eliminated because of a lack of time.

4. **Create incentives/disincentives:** Make a list of all the anticipated household expenses and factor in surplus money to "dig the well." Agree in advance on the consequences of going into too much debt for unnecessary items.

5. **Clearly communicate:** As a family, discuss the expectations of everyone to make the new working scenario a success.

Child

1. **Problem recognition:** Your child is forgetting to take completed homework to school.

2. **Desired outcome:** After your child works hard on homework, you want the teacher to see it and not have it stay in your child's room all day.

3. **Increase capacity/Decrease choice:** Create one large checklist where a child has to record all homework assignments. This serves as the master list of all assignments going back to school.

4. **Create incentives/disincentives:** A child cannot go to bed until all the homework due the next day is checked off and shows it placed inside their backpack. The backpack is then closed and placed next to the front door.

5. **Clearly communicate:** Together with your child, create a written statement, mutually signed, that clearly spells out the process along with any agreed upon consequences.

A Note from Bill

Pay attention to this one! It will make a HUGE difference in your life. Learn to "Change the Circumstances". It could be a quick-fix for a *Change It!* problem. And, it not only works for other people, it works for the change agent as well.

For example, I wanted to start watching less television, and start doing more things that would bring long-term benefits to my family. (This happened about 15 years ago, when I first made the decision to change my life.) I hung a sign on the front of my television that read "I thought you wanted to be free?" When I thought about sitting down in my favorite chair to watch a show, I had to physically lift the sign out of the way to do it! As you can imagine, this made a big difference in my life.

It didn't work every time, but it sure made me think about the television show before I started watching it. The biggest impact came in the avoidance of "habitual television" watching. You know what this is. It is what too many Americans do (and what I did all the time). After dinner, many people just "turn on the tube" and keep switching channels until they find something to watch. This is a habit.

After hanging the sign on the television, my habitual television watching really changed. I had to ask myself "Is there something I really *want* to watch? Is it worth trading my success for this show?" If I couldn't answer "yes" to these questions, I didn't turn on the set.

CHAPTER 8

Helping Others Change

~

SOMETIMES, ALL IT TAKES is a simple question. When Bill Quain was in his forties, one of his students asked him, "Professor, what do *you* want out of life?"

Bill was stunned. No one had ever asked him what he wanted before! Instead, everyone was busy telling Bill what they wanted from him. And while Dr. Quain had no immediate answer to the young man's question, he quickly took action to decide exactly what he did want and how he would get it.

The *Change It!* Program is designed specifically for complicated situations that require a critical shift in thinking and actions. It is a step-by-step process that really works. If you want to create change— and we are talking about really critical and lasting change—you need to invest time with people to help them. There are no shortcuts. Each step is critical.

Unfortunately, the *Change It!* Program doesn't work every time or with every person. But it is the best tool you now have. It is the best tool we have, and we have been working on this area for some time. If you apply it diligently, you can really increase your chances of success.

Remember, as always, we are talking about change for success, not change for the sake of change. We already showed you the consequences of missing *any* of these six steps. Here they are again, and then we will discuss how each one is important when you change others.

1. Problem Recognition
2. Shared Dream

3. Incentive to change

4. Pressure to change

5. Capacity to change

6. Actionable first steps

These are the steps of a program. This program is like any other—it has a flow, a structure, and a purpose. You need to honor the program.

When to Use the *Change It!* Program

In the last chapter, we showed you how to change circumstances in order to get people to make changes in *controlled* situations. We used the Starbucks example to demonstrate what simple change would look like.

You need to use the *Change It!* Program for more complicated situations, involving people over whom you have little control. Here are some examples of situations where the *Change It!* Program is useful.

1. A friend of ours is the CEO of an investment bank and his employees are high-powered investment bankers. These people are very wealthy, so it is impossible to just tell them to do something and expect it to happen. Our friend views himself as a problem solver for his employees. They come to him with problems, and he organizes teams to solve the problems. In some cases, as the leader, he identifies the problem. He then asks them to come up with solutions. His job is to make sure the teams have all the resources they need to get the job done.

2. Bill Quain works with a number of Direct Selling companies. The independent distributors in these companies expand their networks by helping other people make money. The *Change It!* Program helps prospects

identify problems, and then provides a framework for keeping the new people on track, and their businesses growing. With these companies "Actionable First Steps" are extremely important.

3. Doug Price works at Destination Marketing Association International which has more than 600 convention and visitor bureaus / destination marketing organizations (DMOs) as members worldwide. The association introduced industry-wide accreditation as a means to assure staff, leadership, and customers that the DMO is following proper practices and performing at an acceptable level. DMOs that achieve the accreditation demonstrate all six steps of the *Change It!* Program.

The *Change It!* Program is ideal for people working in teams. If you have the opportunity to use it, make sure you share the process with the people on your team. Show them all the steps and talk about the consequences of missing a step.

Step One: Problem Recognition

We discussed Problem Recognition earlier in Chapter 2. But, now we are applying it to *changing others*. Remember, *they* have to identify the problem. You can't just tell them about it.

Sometimes, it is possible to combine Problem Recognition with Shared Dreams. Here is an example:

Two couples go on a short vacation together. Couple A has a strong relationship. They are committed to each other and it shows. Couple B spends a lot of time arguing about little things. Neither one of the people in Couple B wants the other to have a victory. At the end of the vacation, Couple B is driving home and they start to talk. "I noticed that they (Couple A) never raised their voices at each other. That was nice," she said. "Would you like to live like that?"

"It sure would be a lot easier," he said. "Do you think we can change after all these years?"

Okay, that is a simplification. And, we know it is unlikely to happen because Couple B probably got lost on the way home, and he didn't want to stop for directions...

But, it is an example of how Problem Recognition and Shared Dreams can sometimes occur at the same time. Remember our definition of Problem Recognition—when a desired state is different than the actual state.

If you want to help people change, help them develop their capacity for Problem Recognition. Notice we said help them *develop* Problem Recognition. You can't tell them. However, you can help change their circumstance when Problem Recognition is inevitable.

Be warned that recognizing a problem exists is often not enough for most people to take action. If they are in a comfort zone where everyone around them has the same problem, it is unlikely they will take action. This is why the Shared Dream is so important.

Step Two: Shared Dream

Don't be confused here. This is not *your* dream. It is *their* dream. Then why do we call it a "Shared Dream?" Because, when you are helping others to change, you need to show them that you share their dream.

Let's contrast this technique to the typical person who develops a dream, then tries to get others to share that dream. He or she wants to get other people to change so he or she can achieve something for themselves. This doesn't work. Most people will not work for your dream. They will only work for their dream.

Folks, we can't stress this enough. Can you understand what we are saying here? If you are the leader or change agent, you need to take time to find out what *other* people want. Then show them that you want it *for them* as well. This takes time! People need to *trust* you. And, this is where many leaders and change agents fall into trouble.

You can't earn trust overnight, but you can lose it in five minutes! People are reluctant to share their dreams with you. They may be afraid you might make fun of them. Or you might not feel that their dreams are appropriate.

Here is a good example:

Mark is the director of a team of people at a large company. He wants his department to run more efficiently because he is paying too much overtime and it is hurting the firm's bottom line—and his bonus! He takes his team to a *Change It!* Program workshop and they all recognize that overtime is a problem. "Why do you think it is a problem?" asks Mark. One brave team member says "I don't get enough time to spend with my family. I spend too much time here working. Projects come in at the last minute and we end up staying at work too late."

This upsets Mark. He thinks to himself, "Wait a minute. We need to be ready to meet every customer request no matter what it takes. I didn't want to hear that. We need to be recognized as world-class leader." His facial expression says it all. Later, when he writes a memo about company loyalty, everyone gets the message. What is the message?

"Don't tell Mark what you are really thinking. Just go along with what he says."

Here is the point. Mark got his dream mixed up with the people who really mattered. If they want to work less overtime because it gets them home with their families sooner, he should be happy. Once he discovers their dreams, he can show them how he shares those dreams *with them*. His dream really doesn't matter to them. But their dreams certainly should matter to him, because if he helps them achieves their dreams, he will get what he wants.

Step Three: The Incentive to Change

Always, always, always tie the incentive to change directly into the shared dream! Did we mention that you should *always* do it?

We aren't saying that the incentive *is* the dream. The incentive should lead to the completion of the dream.

For example, Sarah is the director of franchisee development for a fast-food company. Currently, the company's restaurants are only open for lunch and dinner, but the company is about to launch a line of breakfast products. This will require many changes! Sarah's job is to sell the franchise owners on the idea and to help them roll out the new concept.

The company has already gone through the Problem Recognition stage. The lack of breakfast items made it difficult for the franchise owners to compete with other chains, and they were also missing opportunities for more revenue. The company spent a long time on the Shared Dream. The franchise owners didn't get into the business so they would have a restaurant. They took all the risks and did all the work so they would have money, and a great lifestyle. In fact, most of the franchisees owned several restaurants in the chain so they would have more opportunities to become wealthy.

Sarah was instrumental in helping to develop some fantastic incentives to encourage franchise owners to make the transition more quickly. For example, any owner who completely implemented the breakfast service in less than 60 days earned a vacation in Hawaii for his or her entire family. This incentive was tied into the Shared Dream of "lifestyle."

Incentives are wonderful. For best results, link them directly to the Shared Dream. Make sure they are meaningful to the person you expect to change.

Are you getting the point? In all of the categories so far, we keep talking about making the problem, the dream, and the incentives relevant to the person you want to change. What you want just doesn't matter to the change targets! The secret for success is to link *their* achievements with your goals.

Step Four: Pressure to Change

You can do some things to put pressure on others. If you are a boss or a parent, pressure will sometimes work. But we are talking about making massive, meaningful, long-lasting and successful changes with and through others. For that, you need to help them develop their own internal pressure technique.

In most cases you cannot put pressure to change on someone else. Why? They will resent you for it. The pressure to change has to come from within *them*. You need to create situations that raise their expectations. This will create the pressure.

How Do You Create Pressure from Within?

This is big time stuff! We are about to let you in on one of the best-kept secrets of modern times. We are going to show you four techniques for creating pressure within a change prospect.

Here are the four strategies:

1. *Stir the pain* – This is a game of "find and remind." Find out what their dream is, and remind them of how great it would be to have it. Do they want more time with their family? Talk with them about it. Do they want vacations? Bring them travel brochures!

2. *Compete against low expectations* – Many people never change because they just don't believe they can. They are stuck. They would "like to have more" but don't believe that "people like me will ever do that." Find some examples of people just like them who have been successful. Give them specific examples.

3. *Motivation through association* – This takes the "overcoming low expectations" model one step further. Get your change prospect around successful people. Let them experience the feeling of successful living. Create a mentor program, but make it clear that there is an end to the program. The idea is to create an incentive to make changes so the change target gets to stay in the successful group.

4. *Create a timeline* – With the "ending date" in mind, map out on a calendar when to realistically accomplish your dream.

Build in logical "milestone dates" in which to measure your progress.

These are *dynamite* techniques. Will they work every time? No. But, how often are you able to effectively get others to change right now?

Step Five: Capacity to Change

Have you ever been asked to make a change, at work for example, but you had no idea what to do? Then, when you finally figure it out, you realize that you don't have the tools you need—training, equipment, money, and so forth. This is a constant, energy-draining problem that causes anxiety and frustration to set in.

Here is a good example:

Yvonne is in trouble. She is way behind in her sales quota. She goes to her sales assistant and says "We need to make some changes around here. Instead of just waiting around taking orders, I want you to start *making* cold calls and doing follow-ups. Get on the phone and make it happen."

The sales assistant is confused. He has no training in cold calling. He is also very busy already and doesn't know where he will get the time to do the cold calls. Finally, he needs some sort of calling list of prospects, and a computer program to manage the sales effort. He tells Yvonne he needs these things.

Yvonne replies "Hey, I am not paying you to ask me questions. We don't have a budget for those things. If we could sell more, we would have the money—" And so forth.

Isn't this familiar? How many great *Change It!* opportunities are lost because the change agent does not give his or her targets the capacity or resources to make changes. Instead, the change agent simply says, "I don't care what you do to get it done, just do it!"

If you want someone to change, you must give that person access to the resources necessary to carry out the plan. This can range from expert advice, to training, to equipment, and more. Expecting or demanding change without developing the capacity will quickly reduce your credibility. It is an excellent way to destroy trust! And remember, once that trust is gone, it is very difficult to rebuild.

The best way to understand the resources necessary to accomplish a change is to first make the change yourself, then ask others to do it. Lead by example!

There is an expression we like for this situation—"A man with experience is never at the mercy of a man with a theory." We first heard this said by Dexter Yeager. Mr. Yeager built a huge company by showing other people how to become successful. But, before Mr. Yeager did any showing, he did a whole lot of *growing*. He did all the work himself first and then asked others to follow him.

Step Six: Actionable First Steps

Question: How do you eat an elephant?

Answer: One bite at a time!

Are you giving your change prospects actionable first steps? Are you showing them how to eat the elephant? Or, are you just telling them to get it done and then letting them be frightened by the size of the task ahead?

Our good friend Carlos is a high school track coach, and also the computer teacher. He is very good at coaching track, and horrible at teaching the computer.

On the track, Carlos specializes in field events, especially the long jump. At the beginning of the season, he takes the new jumpers over to the pit, and tells them "I want you to get used to running down the track, and hitting that take-off spot. Don't worry about how far you are jumping; just get the feel of the track."

He then takes each jumper, one-by-one, walks them to the top of the track, and runs along next to them and yells "jump" just at the right time. Soon, these jumpers have confidence in their ability to hit the jump mark and they can turn their attention to getting some distance.

However, his computer class is not so ideal. On the first day, Coach Carlos sits at his desk, with his feet up, reading *Sports Illustrated* as the students file in. He says "The computers are over there. There will be a test in two weeks, and at the end of the month, you need to develop a website and publish it."

What is the difference? Coach Carlos helps his jumpers *get started* with small steps. He clearly defines the *parts* of the task, not just the entire end result!

Folks, this is an important element in any kind of *Change It!* Program. It doesn't matter if you are trying to earn more money, build stronger relationships, develop a better physical regimen, or build an aircraft carrier! People don't want to face a huge task. They want to get started and have success along the way.

REWARD PLATEAUS

Along with the Actionable First steps, establish achievable first goals, and couple them with desirable first rewards. Why wait until the end of the project to start handing out rewards? Be bountiful!

Look, we aren't suggesting you simply divide the final reward into smaller pieces and give it out as you go along. We are suggesting that you devise some sort of recognition system that gives your change prospects a feeling of milestone accomplishment.

The rewards should escalate as the task goes on. Make sure that their rewards aren't so large that they settle for a portion of the rewards, and stop making achievements towards the completion of the change.

This chapter is designed for you to help others change by using the *Change It!* Program. The examples here should give you confidence to use the system whether dealing with personal change or change in the workplace.

Note from Bill and Doug

We are talking about "creating pressure from within." This is so misunderstood. In fact, most people get it completely wrong: they think they can create pressure from the outside. Well, this does work sometimes. For example, telling someone that they will be fired if they don't change can and does work. But it only works if you have direct control over that person. Even then, it may be temporary, and must be repeated often. The danger is, it can lose its effectiveness over time—especially if no one ever gets fired.

Creating pressure from within, with one of the four techniques we teach here, is a master stroke. It makes life so much easier and is more effective in the long run. Creating pressure from within is like lighting a fire. Then, it is merely a matter of adding more fuel from time to time.

∾ Part III – Change Everything

In many ways, Part III is a How-To section. You have learned to change yourself in Part I, and how to change others in Part II. Now you will learn how to put all the learning into actionable strategies. Does that sound familiar? It should. It follows the *Change It!* Model.

We established the Problems you face, and, with our discussion of success (Money, Sunny and Honey) we stimulated your dream. By telling you that Change is Choice, and especially that Change is *your* Choice, we initiated internal pressure to change. Certainly, the knowledge you gained from this book has increased your Capacity to Change!

So it is time for those Actionable First Steps. It is time to learn EXACTLY how to get started, and to continue, with change. At the end of Part III, you will not only know how to initiate a *Change It!* Program, you will also know how to sell it to others by creating a tangible, meaningful dream for them.

Defining Innovation

$\backsim$

IN HIS FANTASTIC BOOK *Innovate or Evaporate*, Dr. Jim Higgins says that innovation isn't just a choice, it is a necessity. Why? Because the environment is always changing around us. Nothing stays the same. If *you* try to remain unchanged, you will soon be obsolete.

This may be unwelcome news for many people. Innovation is difficult and tiring. It means you have to think creatively—and that is a challenge most of us don't want to face each day. Unfortunately, it is necessary.

When we discuss creative problem solving through innovation, many people say, "I am pretty creative. I can come up with all kinds of ideas. They just don't seem to go anywhere." Well, there is a big difference between creativity and innovation. Dr. Higgins describes it this way:

"Creativity is producing something new. Innovation is producing something new that works!"

You see, it isn't enough to be creative. You must be innovative. In other words, you need to find new ideas that work, not just new ideas.

THE DOT-COM BUBBLE

In the late 1990's, we had a perfect example of the difference between creativity and innovation. In those days, thousands of new companies launched internet business plans. Investors were throwing money at the new ventures. Many internet millionaires turned into internet billionaires overnight. Initial public offerings (IPO's) produced fantastic wealth for the new breed of entrepreneurs.

There was only one problem with these new companies. They didn't actually *do* anything! Yes, there were great ideas, but they didn't have viable business plans. There was no compelling selling proposition. No one was spending any money—except to buy stock.

While the Dot-Com bubble is a great example, the Pets.com website is possibly the best of the best. Do you remember Pets.com? It was an online store to buy pet food and supplies. Their logo and slogan have now become icons for business failure. Their major image was a dog sock-puppet. And their slogan was "Pets.com, because pets can't shop."

Ironically, that dog-sock puppet now shows up in commercials for the new breed of internet retailers. It was such a stunning disaster that it now serves as a reminder that every business, even internet business, needs a viable model to work.

All of those early internet businesses were creative. They were a new idea. But, most of them were not innovative. They didn't work. There was no viable business plan or model.

THE EXCEPTION PROVES THE RULE

Of course, some businesses did survive the crash. Amazon.com is an example of a company that went beyond creativity and innovated a new business model. Amazon is the model for many successful businesses today. They don't sell their own products. Instead, they simply *represent* products.

Author Bill Quain has a high ranking book on Amazon and has sold many books there. Because he started with Amazon in its early days, and because his books sold well there, every new book he writes is sold on Amazon—including this one.

But Amazon doesn't keep Bill's books in inventory. Instead, they order them as they are needed. Bill's publishing company gets a notice from Amazon when the orders come in, and then they send out the needed books.

This is an innovation that helps Amazon make money but keeps their inventory costs to a minimum. Amazon has hundreds of thousands of products for sale. Can you imagine how expensive it would be to keep them all in inventory? As a matter of fact, Amazon once ran a clever advertising campaign about trying to buy the massive Pentagon building with all its 17 miles of hallways to hold their entire inventory!

Using the power of the internet, Amazon has become a major player in the online retail world. Their business model serves as a benchmark for almost all other companies on the web. That is innovation.

A Double Irony

If Pets.com were still around today, it might actually be successful. You see, something happened between the time of the Dot-Com bust and today. People began to shop online more and more. In the early days, there were many difficulties with shopping online. For one thing, people just didn't know how to do it. They had no point of reference. In addition, most people used dial-up internet access in those days. Shopping online was confusing and time-consuming— two things that today's internet merchants have largely overcome.

Now it was possible that pet owners *would* shop online for pet supplies. But in order to be successful, Pets.com would need to do more than just supply shopping items. They would need to inform and educate people on pet-related issues. This information-added aspect is part of the new business model. Now, you can buy practically any sort of pet supply or product you could ever want—you guessed it—on Amazon.

Are you beginning to get the difference between creativity and true innovation? Innovators look for trends and then find new solutions that really work. They don't just start making new stuff or systems. They innovate to solve problems better.

And, here is a big clue for all of us:

While innovators create something new, they do it to solve existing problems!

If you come up with a solution to a problem that doesn't exist yet, that is creative, but not much use to anyone.

A Lesson for *Change It!* Agents

Here's an insight to be gained from the Dot-Com bust. Don't innovate beyond the capabilities of the change targets. It will only lead to failure. Yes, technology is wonderful, and new ideas are great. However, if change is beyond the capacity of your prospects to follow the new idea to completion, you are asking for trouble.

Sometimes, new ideas or techniques are just too radical. You may need to introduce changes in stages, particularly when it involves innovation.

Innovation is Not Problem Recognition

This brings us to an important point in innovation. Look at where the innovation chapters fall in this book. Innovation is a way to carry out the *Change It!* strategies. Innovation is not the *reason* you change, *it is the way you may choose to change.*

Innovation is not Problem Recognition, and it is not Shared Dreams. Those are completely different animals.

It happens all the time to a leader or a change agent who sees something new and thinks "Wow, we must have that technology." Or they notice a competitor or a market leader doing something and think, "We have to do it that way."

This happens in business, and it happens in personal relationships as well. Families often fall into this trap. They see something new and decide, "We should do that." It doesn't seem to matter that the innovation doesn't solve a problem. In fact, implementing new strategies will often cause problems.

In this book, we have been painstaking in our efforts to give you information in a certain way. We built this book to help you go through a process. There is a good reason why innovation is at the end of the book. It belongs there!

You need to go through the stages of change in the correct order. First comes Problem Recognition. Second is the Shared Dream. Only after those things are firmly established should you introduce the strategies for changing the situation.

Next, let's look at three choices you have: do nothing, innovate, or duplicate.

DOING NOTHING IS STILL A STRATEGY

One strategy is to do nothing, even if you see something new and exciting. Have you heard the Hippocratic oath? First, do no harm! If the new thing does not solve an *existing* problem, then don't implement it. Stay away from it. It is better to do nothing than to make innovations that do not solve a problem.

Folks, nothing happens in a vacuum. If you make one change, it is going to impact other things. It is like squeezing one end of a tube of toothpaste! It is the called "The Law of Unintended Consequences."

Did you ever take an action that caused an unintended consequence that you didn't anticipate? Here is a simple example for you. In an effort to feed birds in the backyard of our home, we substituted corn cobs for bird seed to save a little money. We never intended on attracting huge crows that feed on corn cobs. That caused us to have to build our very own scarecrow in the backyard of our home!

INNOVATION INCREASES CAPACITY

A second choice you have is to innovate to increase capacity. Here is a good thought to carry with you. Innovation is capacity, not the Problem Recognition. It is the way you carry out the change. It helps people to implement a strategy to solve a problem.

For example, if you see something new, it may *trigger* the recognition of a problem. But seeing an innovation in action may also enhance your capacity to change, because you now recognize that there is a solution for the problem.

We see this all the time in the Direct Selling industry. Many Direct Selling companies have embraced the internet to help people build businesses. As new people see the innovations, they may realize they have a problem—they aren't making enough money on their jobs, for example. But they also view the innovation as a way to solve that problem. In other words, they now have confidence that the problem can be solved! This increases their capacity to change.

INNOVATION *IS* CAPACITY

Innovation improves capacity to change. For example, many large companies use a technique called *benchmarking* to identify possible innovative techniques. To benchmark, one company will visit the facilities of another, non-competing company to identify new techniques that are successful. In the United States, L.L. Bean, a clothing distributor, is visited so often that they actually have a staff of people just to handle the demand.

Why does L.L. Bean go through the time and expense of being a benchmarked company? Because once people visit, they in fact become a valued customer!

L.L. Bean developed innovative approaches to filling mail-order demand for their huge line of clothing and outdoor gear. Other companies, who do not compete with L.L. Bean, often request a visit to the warehouse to see how they fill orders quickly and efficiently.

For example, a restaurant supply company does not compete with L.L. Bean. But, the restaurant supply company has many of the same problems. They need to store vast quantities of inventory, then receive complicated orders, and fill them. Suppose the restaurant supply company has a recognized problem—their orders are going out too slowly.

They may request a benchmarking visit to L.L. Bean. During the visit, it soon becomes apparent that Bean has solved the problem with innovative order tracking and fulfillment techniques. This gives the executives from the restaurant supply company confidence. They know if they can just adapt the Bean techniques to their own warehouses, they will solve the problem. Also as stated earlier, as new L.L. Bean customers, they have the first-hand knowledge and confidence that their personal orders will be efficiently fulfilled.

This confidence, and the new knowledge, increases the capacity of the restaurant supply company to change. Innovation increases capacity.

People will also benchmark for personal reasons. Many times you will benchmark your own stock portfolio against the S&P 500 and make adjustments accordingly. This knowledge of the stock market can also increase your capacity.

DUPLICATION CAN BE INNOVATION

A third choice you have is to duplicate. It doesn't matter if the innovation is yours or someone else's—unless, of course, it is protected by law, as in a patent or trademark. Use innovations where ever you find them. And, duplicated innovations are often easier to use, because they show your change prospects that it can be done. Again, this adds to your capacity to change.

Duplication can be when a company sees a service offered on a website that they believe their customers would benefit from. As an example, most convention and visitor bureaus offer maps of their destinations online. This is a benefit to visitors, duplicated around the world.

Note from Bill and Doug

We give people some interesting perspectives on innovation versus creativity here. But, we want to make sure we hammer home one important point. Even the most successful innovation needs careful and sustained follow-up and implementation in order to succeed. We see too many people who jump from one thing to the next, without ever really doing the hard work of implementation.

As you know, this is one of our great challenges. We love innovating new ideas. Sometimes, however, we have to put off a new idea because the last dozen or so are still working through the system. It is tempting to turn our attention to the next project before completing the previous ones. Innovating is fun. Changing is hard work!

Be steadfast and thorough. If you have something good—a genuine innovation—make sure it has the chance to become a fully implemented change.

CHAPTER 10

Creative Problem Solving

∽

THE PROCESS OF MOTIVATION IS A COMBINATION of creative problem solving and selling intangibles. You must have both of these factors in order to succeed. In the previous chapter, we discussed the difference between innovation and creativity. Now, in this chapter, we will show you how to pass the creativity barrier and go straight to implementing your ideas.

Very few changes are made alone. Almost all of them involve other people. Look at the three things we want to help you achieve— Money, Sunny and Honey. Do you need to work with other people to get these things? It is difficult to imagine too many worthwhile life experiences that do not involve others. Certainly, relationships require at least two people! And, try making money without encountering customers! Finally, what kind of mental stability would you have if you did not work and play well with others?

When we innovate, we must convince others to work with us. Let's review the first two parts of the *Change It!* Program with this in mind:

Problem Recognition – How many times have we stressed that you must help everyone involved in the change process come to the same problem recognition?

Shared Dream – How do you get people to share your dream? You have to sell them on it.

ESCAPING THE MAZE

Take a look at the following figure. It is from James Higgins's book *Escape from the Maze*. Dr. Higgins is one of the world's foremost experts on creative problem solving and innovation.

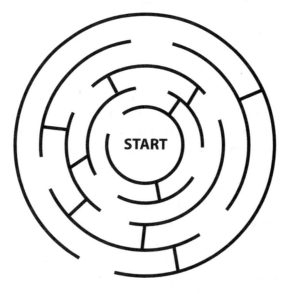

Exercise – Take a pencil and try to escape from this maze. You have 20 seconds.

How did you do? Did you escape from the maze? How did you do it?

Most people (99.9% of us) try to escape by drawing a line with the pencil that never touches one of the lines on the page. If they come to a dead end, they go back, very neatly, and look for another path through the maze.

What a waste of time. Why are you trying to do the same thing you always do? Why do the same thing everyone else is doing?

Here are our suggestions:

1. Start in the center, hold your pencil in your fist, and draw a straight line right out of the maze.

2. Get some dynamite and blow the maze apart first, then walk out.

3. Hire a helicopter and have it pick you up and drop you outside the maze. While you are up there in the helicopter, go someplace really fancy for lunch.

Actually, we learned these solutions from Dr. Higgins, and our lives have never been the same!

Folks, let's get creative! Why do the same thing that everyone else is doing? You need to make changes, not follow the pack.

DON'T GET BLOCKED

Here is the problem. You are not letting your mind get wild. You are bound by all the conventional blockers that have held you back for your whole life. You need to think differently.

We won't go into all the blockers that are preventing you from making the important changes you need. But, here are just a few to think about.

1. **Tradition** – a habit or custom to think this way

2. **Fear** – panic or apprehension set in

3. **Boredom** – caught up in monotony

4. **Low confidence** – lack of self assurance

CREATIVE PROBLEM SOLVING TECHNIQUES

We are so tired of the term "thinking outside the box." It is so overused, that it is almost meaningless today. Instead of thinking outside the box, why not just *stay* outside? Or, better yet, demolish the box.

The world has such great possibility for the bold, the fearless, and the innovative. Your creative mind is just waiting to be unleashed.

We don't have the space in this book to cover the many problem solving techniques available. However, you can find a whole lot of them in *101 Creative Problem Solving Techniques* by our favorite innovation strategist James Higgins.

BRAINSTORMING

For the sake of clarity, however, we do want to cover one technique. It is called *brainstorming* and is used for both personal problem solving, and business applications.

Brainstorming is a group technique. It is very easy—to do incorrectly! Most people make one of two mistakes.

First, they tend to shoot down ideas before they can lead to solutions. Second, they make the mistake of involving a leader who is not open-minded, with a history of killing ideas.

In a brainstorming session, everyone is equal. If you are trying to brainstorm for business, get rid of the bosses for awhile. Why? Because the boss's subordinates will naturally defer to the boss's judgment. It is a real idea killer.

Bill Quain had an experience one time that illustrates the point. He was in a faculty meeting at the University of New Orleans when he was a young, inexperienced professor. The Vice President of the university made an announcement to a large group of faculty.

"Great news," he said. "We are adding three new stories to the library."

"That's great," said Professor Quain. "Who wrote them?"

Everyone thought this was hilarious—for about half a second! Then, they noticed how red the VP's face had become. Suddenly, the room was very silent. Needless to say, Dr. Quain was in trouble!

The same thing happens when a boss is in a brainstorming session.

It simply kills creative thought. Everyone must be free to speak his or her mind.

Here are the basics of how to run a brainstorming session:

1. Gather a group of people, and select a facilitator.
2. Clearly state the problem you wish to solve.
3. Ask people to start calling out ideas.
4. Write every idea on a large piece of paper, and post it on the wall.
5. When an idea is posted, encourage others to use it as a springboard for even more ideas.
6. Keep going until everyone has run out of ideas.

The aim of brainstorming is to *generate* ideas, not *evaluate* them. Don't make any comments—positive or negative—about any idea that comes up. The idea is to create more ideas, not pass judgment.

Generating ideas from other ideas is called *branching*. Branching is an extremely important part of brainstorming. It is amazing how people's minds open up when they are in the presence of free-ranging ideas.

Branching is a very successful technique within brainstorming. Use it whenever you can.

When the brainstorming session is over, there will be plenty of time to evaluate the effectiveness of an idea. There are plenty of people who can do that. The most important task is to be creative.

TURNING CREATIVE IDEAS INTO INNOVATION

Most of the ideas generated in a brainstorming session will not be practical. That doesn't matter. If you don't create a free-wheeling atmosphere, you won't get enough ideas to look through.

Once the ideas are out there, it is time to look for those you can implement. This is the process of turning creativity into innovation. It is a matter of applying constraints and practicalities to the ideas.

Some ideas will be thrown out because of budget constraints. Others will create additional problems, and therefore, are not suitable. Still others will fall short of the complete solution.

Can you see why it is so important to create many ideas? Most of them will not work to solve your problem. But the one that does will set you free!

WHERE (AND WHAT) TO INNOVATE

In any situation, whether it is personal or business, we suggest four areas to look at for innovation. They are Product, Process, Promotions, and People. Let's look at each of them.

Product – You may be confused how a "product" can be a personal item, not just a business item. You are a product! If you want more Money, Sunny and Honey, you need to create the best product you can. In a business sense, products are those things we sell to our customers that solve a customer's problem. It is an excellent area for innovation. You don't need to create brand new products. You can innovate changes in existing products.

Process – This is how we get things done. In business, it may be the way we keep track of things, do reports, produce goods, and so forth. This is a very fertile area for innovation. Brainstorming works very, very well for process innovation. Why? Because the people who are involved in the process are excellent sources for ideas on how to improve it. Again, remember, we are looking for things that serve the customer better, more efficiently, and that make the job easier for those involved.

Earlier in Chapter 7 we pointed to the Starbucks Coffee situational change as a good example of process innovation.

In your personal life, process is also important. How you do things makes a big difference in how much you get done. Are you efficient, a procrastinator, or a whiner? Your procedures for processing all the things in your life will definitely affect your Money, Sunny and Honey.

Promotions – This is a process of communicating benefits. Are you telling the story you want to deliver? Do people understand your role in their life? Innovating in promotions is important in every aspect of your life. Look for better ways to communicate.

People – Who is in your life? What are they doing there? Are you helping them? Or, are you taking from them? Organize the people in your life so that you have a network of people who you can learn from as well as people you can help grow. You want to give, and you want to *get*. So does everyone else. Look for ways to improve your network of friends, family, associates and acquaintances.

All these different aspects of creative problem solving are just the first part in developing true innovation. In the next chapter, we will talk about the second part of innovation—selling intangibles.

Note from Bill and Doug

When people begin to read this chapter, they may think "Wait a minute, in the last chapter, you just said that creativity and innovation are not the same. Now, in this chapter, you are telling me to be creative in order to succeed. Which is it?"

It is important to point out that we are talking about *creative problem solving* in this chapter. Notice the words "problem solving"? Creative Problem Solving is a response to Problem Recognition. It is a series of techniques, leading to an innovation.

CHAPTER 11

Selling Intangibles

❧

HERE IS THE SITUATION. You have identified the problem and developed and shared the dream. You have a vision. You are excited. You are ready to make the change and start reaping the rewards. But then nothing happens. Why?

How many times has this occurred? You just can't seem to get started. You really want to make the changes, but neither you nor anyone else has the energy or enthusiasm to do the hard work to get it done.

One of the biggest problems that we see is that you have not "sold" the concept—to yourself or others. Selling is hard. Most people try to avoid having to be a salesperson because they have a negative image of selling and it shows!

THE *CHANGE IT!* AGENT AS A SALESPERSON

A *Change It!* Agent is a salesperson—in every sense of the word. Now, that may be bad news for you. You may not want to sell. But the truth is that changing is selling. Here is why:

1. Sales people have a product or service. They know the product.

2. The job of the sales person is to identify people with a problem and then solve that problem.

3. Salespeople solve problems with their products.

4. The job of the salesperson is to help the customer see the problem, then get them to take action.

5. The action that a salesperson wants their prospects to take is to buy, and use their product or service.

6. In addition to selling the product, the salesperson helps the prospect to use the product so that they get the most value or benefit.

7. A good salesperson checks back with the new *customer* after the sale to make sure that all is going well and for referrals of new customers.

Sales people solve problems. *Change It!* Agents solve problems.

Sales people have a product or service. *Change It!* Agents have a product or service—the change itself!

Sales people show their customers how to use the product. *Change It!* Agents show their prospects how to implement the change and achieve rewards—the dream!

YOU ARE YOUR FIRST PROSPECT

When you become a *Change It!* Agent, you are your first customer. You need to sell yourself on the idea. Unless you are totally convinced, totally committed to the change, you will never be able to sell it to others.

This requires some self-examination. It requires introspection—knowing and admitting your strengths and weaknesses.

What kind of person are you? Do you believe in "Ready, Aim, Fire" or "Ready, Fire, Aim"? Either one can work!... It all depends on you!

Can you totally commit to an idea or are you the kind of person who is reluctant to make that commitment? Are you cautious, daring, exuberant, and willing? All of these characteristics will affect your ability to convince yourself that you are on the right track. And all of these will trigger reactions from your prospects.

There is an old Irish proverb that sums it up:

"Give us the gift
The Gifted gives us
To see ourselves
As others see us."

If you have a reputation as someone who gets very excited about an idea and then drops it, it will be very difficult to sell others on your commitment. On the other hand, if you are seen as a bully, a control freak, you may get the *appearance* of acceptance of your idea, but no real commitment from your prospects.

In order to sell others, you must sell yourself on the idea first, and then make a total commitment to it. This means you must carefully choose your *Change It!* strategies. Only initiate the very important ones. Commit to them. Stake your reputation on them. Then, help others feel confident in your commitment—to both the idea of change and to the success of your prospects.

You are the change in the eyes of your prospects. The bigger the change, the harder it is for people to separate you and your past history from the actions you want them to take.

Sell the idea to yourself first, and then sell yourself, along with the idea.

SELLING INTANGIBLES

Okay, we have established that ideas are intangibles. They are not hard products that you can see or touch. So selling them is more difficult than selling a hard product.

If you go to the store to buy a television set, for example, you can ask the salesperson to show you a picture on the television. You can watch the television, side by side, with competitive models, and compare the output. You can compare the features of each make and model as well as their prices. You know exactly what you are buying.

Now, television sets are tangible. You can see them, touch them, and test them. Ideas (such as the idea to change) are not tangible. You can't compare them as easily. And they are more dependent on the people who are involved.

In order to successfully sell intangibles, you need to overcome the problems caused by intangibility. The most prominent of these problems is risk. Most people hate risk. It makes them feel uneasy and afraid.

We have already discussed risk at length in this book. People are afraid because they might lose something. It could be time or money or reputation. But it doesn't matter what they are afraid to lose. People just hate risk.

In order to sell an intangible, you must make it tangible! It is that simple. When selling people on change, you need to give them solid evidence that the change can, first of all, solve their problem, and, secondly, be accomplished.

CREATING TANGIBILITY

Both Bill and Doug are *very* familiar with creating tangibility. Both of them have long histories in selling ideas. Bill was the director of restaurant recruiting and service for the Miami, FL, South Beach Wine & Food Festival. His job was to recruit over 100 restaurants to come to a tent on South Beach and give away 3,000 portions of high quality food. And the restaurants did this for free! To make it more difficult, Bill came to the Festival after a very bad year. So not only did he have to convince the restaurants to give away all that food, he had to show them that the mistakes of the past were just that—in the past.

Doug was a senior Vice President of sales for Marriott Hotels. Their sales people sold meeting space for conventions, weddings, and other events. His job was to train people how to sell empty sleeping rooms and meeting space—and charge a lot of money for it!

Both authors know how to create tangibility. Follow their example when selling ideas for change.

Four Techniques to Increase Tangibility

Here are four techniques ANYONE can use to help sell ideas:

1. *High Quality Contact Points* – Give all your *Change It!* programs a name and a brand identity. How? Make every contact point for the *Change It!* strategy a high quality experience. We suggest creating a web page or at least a blog or online forum where ideas can be exchanged. Name your program and put that name prominently at the top of each blog or web page. This gives the project a life of its own.

2. *Warranties and Guarantees* – When American cars were losing market share to Japanese imports, the Americans began making a better, more reliable car. But people were still reluctant to believe that the quality was better. So the Americans began to extend their warranties. This reduced risk and improved sales.

   Do the same thing with your *Change It!* programs. Give your personal guarantee. If you are working with employees, guarantee that they will not be punished if things go wrong. If you are working with other independent business people, give them your personal guarantee that you will work with them. Make it count. If you are introducing a third-party product into the *Change It!* Program, make sure it has a guarantee or warranty.

3. *Provide Credible Examples* – Get testimonials from credible sources. Make sure the testimonials come from people that your prospects will respect, and relate to. Both Bill and Doug used this technique quite successfully. Bill recruited successful restaurant operators to help sell space to other restaurateurs at the Festival. Doug encourages sales people to maximize customer referrals as a valued form of word-of-mouth advertising.

4. *Associate with Successful People* – Do you want others to believe you are a dependable *Change It!* Agent? Start associating with successful people. *Look* like you know what you are doing. *Feel* like you know what you are doing. You get the picture. Get around successful people and stay there. Do you want to have great relationships? Then get away from people who are unsuccessful in that area. Do you want to change your financial fortunes by working with others? Then start associating with financially successful people. Don't let your prospects see you with unsuccessful people.

FIT THE MESSAGE AND THE MODEL TO THE TARGET

Steve Price (no relation to Doug!) was the Vice President of a very successful publishing and training firm in Tampa, Florida. He has a message about selling:

"If you want to convince somebody of something, tell them what they already believe."

We love this, because it is absolutely true. People don't change their minds very often. Instead, they tend to stick to what they already believe. So tell them what they believe.

You do this by letting them discover the message. People respond to a message according to their basic personality type. So, if you deliver your message in a way they like to get it, they are more likely to believe it is what they already believe.

Does that sound complicated? Yet it goes to the fundamental aspect of selling intangibles. Deliver the message in such a way that it seems like the message they already believed.

To do this, you need to understand how people "hear" messages. Research shows that only 7% of communication comes from spoken words; 38% from tone of voice, and 55% from your body language.

Pay close attention to how you are communicating to your targets. As reminder of a good resource from Chapter 6, go back and review the four personality types to help reinforce communication targets.

Summary—Selling Intangibles

Too many great *Change It!* ideas and strategies have died prematurely because no one took the time to sell them to the targets. Your *Change It!* prospects are like customers. They are people with problems. You have solutions. You want them to take action with *your* solutions.

However, in order to sell other people, you must first sell yourself. This means knowing your strengths and weaknesses, and especially, knowing how other people see you. If you have a reputation for coming up with ideas, then not following through, you will have to sell yourself first, and then sell the idea. As a resource for selling in general, see Doug Price's book *License to Sell*.

On the other hand, if you have spent a lifetime serving as a good example, you can use that image to reduce risk and sell people on your ideas.

Finally, know how to present information to people. Everyone has a basic personality type—including you. The trick is to adjust your personality to meet the needs of the situation. Imitate the chameleon and change with your customers.

Once you learn to sell your ideas, you will find a great deal of success with the *Change It!* Program.

Notes from Bill and Doug

A few words about risk. People hate risk. No one really likes it. Yet risk is necessary for rewards.

Our entire capitalist system is based on a series of risks and rewards. The greater the risk, the greater the rewards should be. But, since most people are risk-averse, the *Change It!* Agent needs to assume more of the risk than the *Change It!* targets. The object is to *grow* targets that are willing to assume more and more risk. Eventually, some members of the team will evolve into more serious risk-takers, making your job as the *Change It!* Agent easier.

But, there are two important things to remember. People only grow as risk takers when they have initial success as a small risk taker. Second, those who take greater risks should receive greater rewards. By using a greater risk/greater reward strategy, you encourage people to grow as risk takers. And, you identify those people who will not grow. Both of these bits of knowledge are extremely important in long-term *Change It!* strategies.

One final word. As the *Change It!* Agent, you are assuming the biggest risk. So, make sure you are rewarded proportionally. Don't take incentives and rewards away from others, but make sure you reach your dreams.

CHAPTER 12

Recap of *Change It!* & Epilogue

༄

THROUGHOUT THE BOOK WE HAVE ATTEMPTED to get across some basic principles concerning change. As a way to recap for you, here are the foundations of the book. Our tip to you back in the beginning was that to get the most out of the book, use this chapter to record the page numbers for each important principle. This way the book becomes a useful resource for you now and in the future.

PAGE

- _____ If you want to change your life, you have to change your life.
- _____ Change is a relatively permanent shift or alteration of *beliefs, attitudes, habits, behaviors or processes* in response to anticipated risks and opportunities.
- _____ Become a winner at the start and don't wait until it's too late.
- _____ Don't make the one-and-done change mistake.
- _____ There is an "I" in *Change It!*

- _____ The *Change It!* Program has six key steps—don't miss one because there are consequences. It all begins with problem recognition. Without it a change dies right away. There is no chance for change to take place if you don't recognize some sort of problem from the very start.

- _____ Dig the well before you need the water.

- _____ True success means having Money, Sunny, and Honey in abundance with balance.

- _____ Money is an important tool and not the root of all evil. The love of money is at the root of all evil.

- _____ Sunny denotes a person with a positive outlook on life. Sunny comes from improving ones physical, mental, and spiritual health.

- _____ Honey refers to successful relationships which are the currency of life.

- _____ It is easier and quicker to change the way you *react* to people (and situations) than it is to *change others*.

- _____ Don't waste your time on things that do not increase your Money, Sunny, or Honey.

- _____ Make big changes at the beginning of a project then prioritize everything in your life to keep your dreams on track.

- _____ You will be able to get some people to change, but not every time.

- _____ Become a change agent who works hard for the good of people who will change.

- _____ Help people change by changing their circumstances.

- _____ Begin with the outcome you want and use the "backwards design" model to force yourself to achieve success.

- _____ Create reward plateaus as tasks are accomplished so you can enjoy success throughout the journey.

- _____ Creativity is producing something new. Innovation is producing something new that works.

- _____ As change agents, don't innovate beyond the capabilities of the change targets.

- _____ Innovation improves capacity to change.

- _____ Doing nothing is a change strategy if something will not solve an existing problem.

- _____ Duplicating can be innovation so long as it's legal to do.

- _____ Be a creative problem solver and don't get blocked from changing.

- _____ Brainstorming is a creative problem solving group technique.

- _____ When innovating, look at your product, process, promotion, and people.

- _____ As a *Change It!* agent, you have to sell your ideas first to yourself and then to others.

- _____ In order to sell something intangible, you must make it tangible thru solid evidence.

- _____ To convince someone of something, tell them what they already believe.

Besides these fundamental principles, we have shared personal experiences with you along the journey. By the time you are reading this book, the following story will be a reality for one of the authors.

Just to show to you how the *Change It!* Program continues to work in our everyday life, read Doug Price's story below.

Problem Recognition

One day while shaving I noticed my upper right cheek bone was swollen and I had never noticed it before. I wondered if it was a bug bite and didn't think much more about it. I asked my wife that same day if she could see it and she certainly could. We kicked around a couple of theories and decided it might be an abscessed tooth although I'd never had one to compare it to. Now that the problem was recognized it was time to act. Though I was not feeling "pain" both of us knew something was not right.

Shared Dream

Once you tell a caring spouse about a problem you are facing, there is no "wishing" it will just go away. Whether you are sharing problems or dreams, there is no turning back when people care for one another. We were going to find out how to deal with this—no big deal!

Incentive to Change

More on this in a few minutes but safe to say we soon learned that "no big deal" would present its own incentives to change!

Capacity to Change

In order to have the knowledge and resources needed to deal with the swelling on my cheek, we indeed had to start asking some tough questions. My dentist quickly determined it was no tooth abscess. He referred me to an oral surgeon who correctly identified it as some sort of tumor and ordered a biopsy. The good news came back that it was benign. The bad news was he was not exactly sure what type of benign tumor we were dealing with. We asked all kinds of questions as to what could it be. How rare is it? What would cause it? If you can't do a full diagnosis, who can? He simply asked us to try and relax, give him a little time to research it and be thankful it was benign!

Pressure to Change

The oral surgeon certainly felt pressure. Once he knew it was benign it helped him determine this tumor was in fact beyond his expertise. For me personally, that proved to be the most important decision to date. He had put pressure on himself to find who could treat this. Through God's grace, he found the most qualified surgeon *in the world* was only a one hour drive away. This was great because I was soon to learn that some of his patients travel from around the world for his care.

Action Steps

We mentioned earlier in the book that the first action steps should be so easy that it is almost impossible not to act. When I learned the most qualified surgeon in the world was one hour away, I was ready to see him that day! Once we eventually met and all the tests determined what type of tumor it was, the action steps fell into place. Back in step three, I mentioned we would learn of our incentives to change. We learned that doing nothing was not an option. I had incentives for a successful long term recovery which meant significant short term sacrifices, but I had options and incentives!

Epilogue

As I write this, my surgery is about to take place. In times like this when change is literally staring you in the mirror, it is comforting to know there is a method to the madness. Also when time allows you to have some input, this *Change It!* Program really works when you need it most.

A Note from Bill

Doug, as usual, you understated the seriousness of your condition. The tumor, although benign, is very threatening. And, as I understand it, you will be in the hospital for several weeks, not just a visit to the dental surgeon's office. However, you did a great job incorporating the *Change It!* Program into the medical situation.

I think it is a great way to end the book. Change is a constant factor in our lives. We can't anticipate the exact circumstances of any change situation, but we certainly can predict that we will need to make changes—some of them radical—throughout our lives.

And, in the end, this is probably the most important message we bring to our readers. "Dig the well before you need the water." Develop a habit of successful strategies that make you less vulnerable to the challenges of life—and just as importantly—put you in the position to take advantage of opportunities.

Be ready, be vigilant. Be an example so that when it comes time to *Change It!* you already have a reputation as someone who can get it done. And remember, if you want to change your life, you have to change your life.

Afterword from Doug Price

My surgical recovery has been a roller coaster ride. On two separate occasions, I have been admitted back into the hospital to battle infections.

I am reminded that this process called "healing" is more of a marathon run than a sprint. Healing has tested my patience, but I know in the long run, I will be grateful to have my good health once again.

I am indebted to Dr. Robert Ord, Dr. Domenick Coletti, and the entire staff of doctors, nurses and assistants at the University of Maryland Medical Center in Baltimore. They are a world-class team in every sense of the word and I thank them for their expertise, dedication, and professionalism.

Finally, a sincere thanks must go to my wife Kathy, who has had to change *her* life to help me change *my* life.

Bill Quain, Ph.D. is the author of 15 books on Personal Growth and Marketing. His books are published in 20 languages, and have sold more than 2 million copies. He is also an award-winning speaker, traveling the world from Europe, to North America, to Asia.

Dr. Quain spent 25 years as a college professor. He was named "Outstanding Teacher" at four Business Colleges. Prior to his teaching career, he worked in the Hospitality Industry. In addition to owning and operating a hotel and restaurant, he was an executive chef.

Bill Quain began to lose his eyesight to Macular Degeneration at the age of 14. This handicap does not slow him down however. In 2001, he became the host of the PBS television show "Cooking Without Looking" - the first cooking show for the blind! In 2005, Oscar-Winning actress Marlee Matlin recruited Bill to serve as a guest consultant and chef for an episode of ABC's *Extreme Makeover Home Edition*.

Bill lives in Ocean City, New Jersey with his wife Jeanne, and their two daughters.

Doug Price is the Senior Vice President of Professional Development for the Destination Marketing Association International (DMAI) in Washington, DC. He is responsible for all education and accreditation functions of the Association. DMAI represents more than 700 Convention and Visitor Bureaus around the world.

Doug is a renowned speaker and consultant, traveling worldwide to deliver presentations to professional audiences. He is the author of 3 books, including *Change It!*, *License to Sell*, and *License to Serve*. His audiences and readers range from corporate directors, to sales people, to highly independent entrepreneurs and business owners. Doug speaks and writes from the heart, based on his years of experience in sales, marketing, and customer service.

He spent 18 years with the Marriot Hotel Corporation, rising to the rank of Vice President. Later, he owned and operated a consulting firm.

Doug resides in northern Virginia, with his wife Kathy, and their daughter. His son is an assistant producer in the television industry, living in California.